Reading Drama

AN ANTHOLOGY OF

PLAYS

ROBERT DiYANNI

TEACHER'S GUIDE

Prepared by

JUDITH A. STANFORD

Rivier College, Nashua, New Hampshire

Macmillan/McGraw-Hill School Publishing Company

Project Editor: Charles Roebuck
Production Supervisor: Diane K. Lindeman
Cover Design: DanielsDesign Inc., New York

Text Development, Design, and Production: Keim Publishing
Designer: Claudia DePolo
Editor: Rita Tomkins

1 2 3 4 5 6 7 8 9 0   DOCDOC   8 9 4 3 2 1 0 9

ISBN 0-07-537506-0

ACKNOWLEDGMENTS

I would like to thank Rebecca Burnett, Carnegie Mellon University, and Kathleen Cain, Merrimack College, for their useful contributions to the sections on *Antigonê* and *Macbeth*; Jeanne Provencher, Nashua High School, for her fine work on *A Raisin in the Sun*; and Henri Forget.

PREFACE

Reading Drama provides an approach to drama that emphasizes the reading process as an active enterprise involving both thought and feeling. While it introduces students to the interpretation of plays through discussion of the elements of drama, it also encourages them to value their previous experiences with life, literature, and theater. Students are invited to consider why they respond to a play as they do and how their responses may change during subsequent readings or viewings. They are encouraged, moreover, to see drama as a significant reflection of life and an imaginative extension of its possibilities.

Reading Drama acknowledges the complex relationship that exists between thinking and feeling when one considers theatrical texts. Chapter One, Reading and Responding, views reading as an art, not a science with rigidly defined rules. The chapter is organized around the theoretical approach to texts outlined in Robert Scholes's *Textual Power* (Yale University Press, 1985). Scholes identifies three aspects of literary response: reading, interpretation, and criticism. In *reading* we attend to our impressions of a text, especially to our preanalytical emotional responses—our subjective reactions. At this stage of reading, we make sense of the play's language and situation in an impressionistic way, filling in gaps in the text and relating the work to our experience. With a second kind of reading, sometimes performed along with the first, sometimes consequent to it, we begin the work of *interpretation*. This more analytical mode of reading involves four aspects: observing details, connecting details, formulating inferences, and drawing conclusions. This process of interpretation is rational, intellectual, and analytical. Following from interpretation and dependent upon it is *evaluation*—what Scholes calls "criticism." I prefer the alternative term, "evaluation," because it lacks the negative judgmental connotation implicit in "criticism." I favor it also because of its richness of implication, encompassing both making judgments about a text and examining the values presented. In this sense, evaluation concerns two things: (1) aesthetic appreciation, a sense of a play's artistic merit; and (2) a response to its moral attitudes and cultural dispositions, whether explicitly articulated or implicitly suggested by the work.

Reading Drama is based on the premise that reading plays requires more than a mechanical skill or a set of rigid rules. Reading, rather, is a deeply humanizing act, an art that stretches the mind while engaging the heart. It is a value-laden and values-evoking experience whose greatest reward—pleasure—is also its most immediate and memorable.

Robert DiYanni

CONTENTS

INTRODUCTION

The format of the Teacher's Guide for *Reading Drama* corresponds to the student text. Chapter One provides additional background information about the three-tiered approach to reading as well as specific suggestions for in-class or homework activities applicable to any of the plays. The chapter ends by concentrating on *The Rising of the Moon*, the play included in the first chapter of the student text. Chapter Two provides additional information about the critical terms introduced in the student text and discusses some supplementary terms as well.

Part Two covers each play individually, beginning with a biography of the playwright. When it is relevant, this is followed by general historical information. Specific information about teaching the play is followed by an act-by-act summary. There are two groups of questions: the Discussion and Writing Topics suggest subjects for in-depth analyses of the major themes and characters in the play; the Going Further questions give students an opportunity to explore more aspects of the play. Answers are provided only for the Discussion and Writing Topics.

Included at the back of this guide is a special section of short biographies of the playwrights. This section can be photocopied and distributed to students as a small reference booklet.

PART ONE

Introduction
to Drama

Reading and Responding

The Pleasures of Drama

This section of Chapter One emphasizes the enjoyment drama brings the reader or viewer and encourages students to value all of their responses, both emotional and intellectual, when they see or read a play. Because much of drama's pleasure comes from its *immediacy*—its ability to render past experience as though it were currently happening—and from its *interactive* nature—the relationships of its characters as they respond to one another—students will gain more from the study of plays if they put themselves in the place of actors. You might introduce drama by giving students some brief background information on *The Rising of the Moon* as preparation for reading the first section aloud. The play takes place while Ireland was under British domination (hence the Sergeant's conflict between his duty to the English-run government and his emotional inclination to support the Irish rebels and their cause). Without this bit of information, many students fail to see the point of the play, even after they have finished reading it. During the first class, you might have students meet in groups of four: three to play Policeman B, Policeman X, and the Sergeant, and one to direct (suggest changes in the readings or offer advice on gestures or movements). After ten minutes or so of practice, each group can present their reading, followed by a general discussion of the differences among the groups' interpretations and whether or not those differences seemed significant. A useful follow-up assignment asks students to finish reading the chapter, including both the rest of the play and the commentary. They might write brief responses both to the drama and to Robert DiYanni's observations. Several of these responses read aloud serve as a logical introduction to the next class meeting.

Some students will be familiar with reading drama, but others who have little experience with the genre may encounter initial difficulties with stage directions and with the characters' names that precede each speech. Some students find these distracting and have trouble following the action of the play while also paying attention to comments on scenery or advice on gestures. Hearing the play read aloud while following along with the script may help overcome this problem. That way the stage directions and characters' names register on the reader/viewer's eyes, but he or she does not actually hear them. It is that dual-level response that the neophyte reader must develop, "seeing" the unspoken parts of the play but "hearing" in the mind's ear only the spoken words. Some students like to read the whole play through, noting the characters' names and reading stage directions carefully but only skimming the dialogue. Then when they return for a second, careful reading of the dialogue, the directions and names fit in almost subconsciously. Discussing previous experiences students have had with reading (or acting in) drama would be useful during the introductory week of study.

As the study of drama continues, consider arranging for the class to see film versions of one or more of the plays they will read. If it is possible to see a staged version, of course, the experience is well worthwhile. Whether you see a film or a live presentation, students will want to discuss the differences between reading a play and seeing it performed and note how the play changed for them after viewing it. You might also discuss the differences between staging and filming: what can each do that the other cannot? Are there certain plays that students believe would be best presented on film rather than on a stage? On a stage rather than on film? Through such discussions, you can stress the *mimetic* (imitative of human experience) and *active* qualities of drama.

As Robert Scholes suggests in *Textual Power* (Yale University Press, 1985), readers begin to find meaning in a text through emotional and subjective responses. *Reading Drama* urges students to heed their early, precritical observations and to learn how those observations can lead to (or sometimes integrate with) interpretation and evaluation. Reading may be presented as an art, not as a mechanical process to be carried out with a standard set of "tools" and a fixed list of rules. Students are encouraged to notice the way their feelings and ideas about a play change when they reread it. Successive readings allow time for the reader to observe details, to make connections among those details, and to develop inferences based on those details and connections. Through this recursive reading, students move from the initial, subjective stage to intellectual, analytic responses.

In judging or evaluating a play, students may respond to its literary and artistic merit as well as to the values, implied or stated, in the work. Students are usually engaged by discussion of a work's values, especially when they consider how those values impinge on their own. As you read *The Rising of the Moon*, you may want to remind students of the importance of integrating feelings and thoughts, analysis and evaluation. Almost certainly you will want to encourage rereading and reconsideration of first responses.

The commentaries included both in the student text and in this guide are not intended as exhaustive interpretations of the plays. We have purposely included open-ended questions and comments to suggest that much of the pleasure of reading comes from formulating one's own responses to what an author has to say and from listening and reacting to the responses of others. Writing and discussion topics are intended as interpretive leads, directions, and approaches that allow students—and their instructors—to develop their own interpretations.

Rather than leading students to agree on definitive interpretations, you may want to encourage them to respond thoughtfully and attentively. Students should become aware of their own reading processes; classwork can provide guidelines, strategies, and model behaviors that will help them become more attentive, reflective, and engaged as they read. The goal is for students to become sensitive to the works and to value their previous experiences of language and life.

As students read Lady Gregory's play in this initial chapter, they learn what we actually *do* as we read. They learn to value their responses, and they develop important steps in the reading process:

observing, connecting, and *inferring*. As we read, we notice details, we see relationships among these details, and we make inferences based on those connections. To become sharp observers and astute thinkers, students need reassurance that reading carefully is not only acceptable but is desirable and necessary. Speed reading has been touted as a solution or an aid to acquiring great stores of information quickly and effectively. And, of course, it does have many important applications. For instance, students should know how to skim newspapers and magazines. Speed reading does not work well, however, for complex texts, whether they be literary, historical, scientific, philosophical, or legal.

When we read texts that are rich with meanings, we need to slow down and allow ourselves time to understand what the writer is saying. We may need to reread a particular passage or sentence several times. We may need to look up a word or check a reference. Students often berate themselves when they read slowly or when they need to reread. Reassure them that slow reading is not necessarily a liability—and is often an asset—by pointing out that they need time to reflect on both *what* writers say and *how* they say it. For particularly difficult sections of the plays, you might suggest that students read so deliberately that they can actually "hear" the sound of the words and the tone of voice that the speaker might use.

In many ways, reading is like having a conversation with a person to whom you wish to—or need to—give your full attention. First, you listen carefully to what the person has to say. While you are listening, you observe the speaker or speakers and note the details of what is being said. You will probably engage in a dialogue in your mind as you hear the speakers' points or arguments develop. While you listen, or later as you contemplate what you have heard, you form inferences. You proceed, usually, to two steps that are also part of the reading process: *interpreting* and *evaluating*.

After students have gathered data by making observations, establishing connections, and drawing inferences, they will be ready to develop conclusions. Interpretation occurs, of course, both while we read and after we read. As students try to make sense of what they have read, to see patterns, and to generate hypotheses, they begin to evaluate the ideas and images they have discovered. Stu-

6

dents—and all readers—compare their own worlds to those of the writers and evaluate the reasonableness of that reconstructed world.

Because they have become involved in the texts they are reading, students will find that their reactions to a playwright's meaning and style are rarely neutral. You can help them to extend their involvement with what they have read by encouraging them to consider the assumptions that underlie the plays and to evaluate those assumptions. As they discover how a text persuades—or fails to persuade—them to a particular view of an experience, event, character, or idea, students may come to a new understanding of the play. By learning to make critical evaluations, students discover that they can accept or reject what an author has written. They need not to be manipulated by the assumptions and values of the writer; instead they can learn to make an analysis that allows them to distance themselves from the work. They move from a subjective response to an objective evaluation and thus place the work in both a personal and a social framework.

As students become more conscious of their own reading processes and more capable of evaluating their reactions to what someone else has written, they will become more aware of their own writing as well—both process and product.

A questioning approach accompanied by open-ended comments encourages students to discover topics that are genuinely interesting to them. When they learn to ask significant questions without worrying about whether or not they discover one "right answer," they will have developed a powerful invention strategy that enables them to become engaged with their writing and to explore subjects worthy of their time.

Reading, Writing, and Thinking About Drama

As you study *Reading Drama* with your students, you should emphasize the relationship between the reading process and the writing process. The appendix to the anthology, "Writing About Drama," offers a comprehensive explanation and introduction. You may find it useful to assign the appendix before students begin to read the plays. In addition to the suggestions given in the appendix, here are some possibilities for integrating writing into the study of drama.

Each of these alternatives offers a way to supplement or replace the formal critique or traditional interpretive paper.

1. *Journals*: If students record their responses to what they have read—as well as to what they hear during lectures and class discussions—they will do a great deal of writing. You might ask them to write two or three one-page entries in response to each play they read. Students may read their journal entries aloud to begin class discussion, or they may use their responses as prewriting for formal papers. In addition, you may want to collect the journals and make brief responses to the students' observations. The suggestions for writing at the end of the "Writing About Drama" anthology appendix can serve as inspiration for journal topics.

2. *Warm-up Writing*: Any of the questions in the student text or in this guide can be used as the subject of a brief writing assignment at the beginning of a class. Students can write for ten or fifteen minutes and then discuss their responses, either in small groups or with the entire class. If you have warm-up writings fairly often, students tend to come to class prepared. In addition, the discussions that follow warm-ups are usually more focused and lively because students have had a chance to think more fully about what they have read.

Some instructors like to inspire (or incite) students by writing a controversial observation about a play on the chalkboard. (For instance, "The Sergeant in *The Rising of the Moon* is an old fool. He risks his career because he has allowed a common criminal to play on sentimental feelings.") Students must then write their responses—before making oral comments. Students may also enjoy the chance to formulate their own controversial comments. You may want to screen these before they are presented to the rest of the class.

3. *In-Class Essay Series*: The in-class essay series requires some organization, but the results are usually worth the effort. In this exercise, students write a series of short essays (perhaps three) on various topics, using part of a different class period for each essay. The essays should be stored all together in a folder. After all three essays have been written and collected (but not corrected by the instructor), redistribute them at the beginning of a class period to the students who wrote them. Meeting in small groups, students

should then share the results of the writing and choose, with the advice of their fellow writers, which of the three essays they will rewrite and resubmit for a grade. Ask them to submit the original essay along with the final copy, so you will have a chance to observe and comment on their revision processes. The questions in this guide provide possibilities for essay subjects.

4. *Review Reports*: As you come to the end of studying drama, each student may prepare a three- to five-minute oral commentary on a play that the class read during the term. The focus of the commentary might be a particularly strong positive or negative response or, even better, an explanation of a changing response. If these reports are presented as part of each class during the final week of the study of drama, they will serve as a basis for review. You might ask students to announce their choices a week in advance to ensure that a fair number of plays are covered. Each student may be asked to submit a one-page summary to accompany the oral commentary.

5. *Student Reviewers*: Early in the term, divide students into teams of four with each team designated to research reviews written about one of the assigned plays. In some instances, students will be able to find both contemporary and modern reviews (for example, with Ibsen's and Yeats's plays). In other cases (the plays of Sophocles and Shakespeare, for instance), it may be difficult or impossible to find contemporary reviews, but modern reviews of specific performances of *Antigonê* or *Macbeth* should be accessible. (The *New York Times Index,* available at most libraries, is a good source to start with.) After reading reviews and developing a "feel" for the vocabulary and style, each team should develop a panel presentation with each "critic" giving both the view of the reviewer whose work he or she read as well as a personal critique of the play. If the class lends itself to a little humor, you might ask students to end each panel with a Siskel-and-Ebert-style "thumbs up/ thumbs down" response to the play in question. Students should also submit their reviews in written form.

6. *Writing and Presenting Drama*: Assign groups of four or five students the task of reading a short story (ideally from an anthology to which all students have access). They should then choose a scene from that story and rewrite it as a scene from a play, in-

cluding stage directions and suggestions for props and settings. Several class periods can be devoted to presentation of the dramatized scenes and discussion of how the short story differs from the play. Students should submit the completed script as a collaborative writing project. (If you are assigning Susan Glaspell's play *Trifles*, this assignment works especially well because Glaspell also wrote a short story version called "A Jury of Her Peers." This story is widely anthologized, and you may want to make a copy available to students as they plan their own "genre conversions.")

7. *Writing Summaries:* To teach students how to summarize accurately, ask them to write a summary of one act of any play in the anthology. This guide provides summaries of each play, so students could then be asked to meet in groups and compare their summaries with a photocopy of the guide's summary. Discussion should address what has been included in each summary, what has been omitted, and what changes students believe would improve either their own summaries or the summary from the guide.

The Rising of the Moon

Isabella Augusta Persse, Lady Gregory (1852–1932)

Isabella Persse was the daughter of a wealthy landowner in County Galway, Ireland. She lived the typical sheltered, privileged life of an upper-class girl during her growing-up years, although she was perhaps atypical in her voracious reading habits. Her father prided himself on his library, and his daughter had free access to whatever books she fancied. At age 28 (rather late for a young woman growing up in Victorian times, when debutantes "came out" at age 18, enjoyed a social season, and were considered successful if they made a "good match" at the end of that year) she married Sir William Gregory, a former governor of Ceylon. After his death in 1892, she edited his memoirs and letters; but more important, she now felt free to become part of the Irish literary scene, opening her home and her life to such Irish writers as W. B. Yeats, James Joyce, and John Synge. Her association with these writers affirmed her desire to reaffirm the native Irish culture that had been rigidly and cruelly repressed since the British domination of Ireland that began in the sixteenth century. Along with Yeats, Synge, and others, Lady Gregory was one of the founders of the Irish National Theatre Society (later housed at the Abbey Theatre) in Dublin. She wrote volumes of Irish folk tales in a significant effort to revive Irish national tradition and wrote plays noted for their accurate transcription of Irish dialect as well as their emphasis on patriotic themes and local myths. Lady Gregory's plays enjoyed great popularity when they were produced at the Abbey. Her dramas nearly always drew standing-room-only crowds while Yeats's and Synge's productions often played to half-full houses. Nevertheless, her literary reputation during her lifetime can best be described as ambiguous. Her willingness to serve as hostess to her fellow playwrights and to handle various aspects of theater management provoked Bernard Shaw to describe her as "the charwoman of the Abbey Theatre," and her plays most admired by contemporary critics were often attributed to others, including Yeats. Fortunately, Lady Gregory's plays have in recent years gained the attention and acclaim they deserve. Her original works, as well as her translation into Irish speech of four plays by Molière (in *The Kiltartan Molière* [Dublin: Maunsel, 1910]), attest to her intellect, wit, and talent.

Teaching the Play

As is mentioned earlier in this guide, students will gain most from this play if they understand the depth of Irish bitterness toward the conquering British who dominated the country until 1914 when Parliament granted home rule to Ireland. Even then, of course, the anger continued because Protestant factions in Northern Ireland, happy with their industrial success and fearful of their religious differences with predominantly Roman Catholic Southern Ireland, asked to be given a separate government. This separate government, connected to the British government, was granted through acts passed in Parliament in 1920 and 1922. Most of Lady Gregory's works, including *The Rising of the Moon,* are set during the period before home rule, when government officials, including police officers, were controlled by and reported to British superiors. An Irish underground, later to become the IRA (Irish Republican Army, organized by Michael Collins after the Easter Rebellion of 1916), actively worked to subvert and sabotage British rule. The young ballad-singer, then, represents much more than a common criminal. He is a political rebel belonging to a group whose actions and goals enjoyed much sympathy among the citizens of Ireland.

You may want to begin discussion by focusing on the conflict within the Sergeant. Students often find his divided loyalties difficult to understand because we do not have an exactly equivalent situation in this country. You might ask them to consider how a police officer today might feel if he or she were called upon to arrest demonstrators who were in violation of a law yet were protesting against a policy which the officer also opposed. Thinking about such similar circumstances will help students to understand the conflicts, risks, and motives of both the Sergeant and the ballad-singer.

Discussion and Writing Topics

1. The play is divided into two parts in the student text: one part is quite short, and the other, longer section comprises the main action—conflict and resolution. What purpose is served by each section?

The first section shows the discussion between the Sergeant and the police officers. We learn the essential details of setting, character, and plot to make the second section meaningful. For example, we learn that the police officers regard the escaped prisoner with awe, and we see the Sergeant as a "law and order" man. The second section builds suspense, leading to the Sergent's conflict when he discovers that the ballad-singer is the wanted man. The Sergeant struggles with his private and public values, and finally, as the climax of the play, makes his decision not to arrest the Man. Because we have seen the Sergeant as a conservative law officer both in the first section and in his conversation with the escaped prisoner, we see his final action as ironic. He makes a decision exactly opposite to what he, and we, expected he would do.

2. What part does irony play in defining the two main characters and their relationship?

Irony, the discrepancy between what is said and what is meant or between what seems to be so and what is so, plays a major role in *The Rising of the Moon*, as is mentioned in the student text. Teaching this play provides the perfect opportunity to introduce this important dramatic concept to students. The relationship between the Sergeant and the ballad-singer is ironic from the beginning. Neither one is what he seems at first to be. The Sergeant upholds a personal rather than a public law; he does not arrest the man who is purported to be a dangerous killer. The Man, on his part, does not live up to his reputation. He seems gentle and playful rather than fierce and mean-spirited. During their conversation, the Sergeant recalls scenes from his boyhood and admits that he can imagine himself as a wanted criminal. When he is able to put himself in the place of the hunted Man, the Sergeant changes radically. The man who has served the state all of his life now sees that he owes allegiance to himself and to his fellow humans, not to an organization in which he cannot believe.

3. *What are the central issues of the play?*

The play takes place in Ireland and the ballad-singer represents the Irish rebels, while the Sergeant represents the Irish who work for the British who keep "law and order" and British rule in place. The play suggests that the powerful and the powerless will someday change places. The actions of the two main characters suggest that the common people will eventually win; there is a sense of optimism and idealism. When the Sergeant asks himself at the end of the play, "[A]m I as great a fool as I think I am?" we realize that the question may well be ironic. He knows—as we know—that in many ways he is not a fool. He is a moral man who has seen his connection with his beginnings and who has acted on that vision.

Going Further

1. *Imagine that you are the Sergeant. Write a series of journal entries, beginning with the night before the one we see in the play. In the first journal entry, describe your reactions to the "Wanted" poster. In subsequent entries, reflect on your meeting with the*

Man, your thoughts and actions as the two of you talked, and your reactions to your decision.

2. Speculate on the reasons why the Sergeant became a police officer rather than a lawbreaker. Are there hints suggesting that he might have become a lawbreaker? What future do you predict for the Sergeant?

3. Create a dialogue between Policeman B and Policeman X as they return to the station.

4. Rewrite the end of the play, beginning with the entrance of Policeman B and Policeman X after they've put up all the placards. Change the situation slightly so that these two policemen stay with Sergeant rather than return to the station.

CHAPTER TWO

Elements of Drama

Chapter Two introduces the critical terms commonly used in the discussion of drama. The terms are explained as an integrated part of reading and responding to plays, and they are illustrated through references to Lady Gregory's *The Rising of the Moon*. If students have not yet read this play (which is part of Chapter One), they should do so before studying Chapter Two. Students should be encouraged to view this specialized vocabulary as a useful and expedient means to express their ideas about the works they read. Although each new term is explained and illustrated when it is introduced, the text stresses that the elements of drama work together. No dramatic element stands by itself, although a particular play may emphasize one specific element more than another play does.

As students begin this chapter, they should be reminded that their emotional and subjective responses must not be pushed aside or relegated to a lesser role. While they are acquiring the vocabulary to write analyses, critical judgments, and literary arguments, they should keep in mind that all good writing begins with honest responses to a topic. In their initial reactions to their reading, they will discover the seeds for their analytic, evaluative papers. And while they are writing a paper, they will want to return again and again to the text of the play they are writing about to see whether their initial thoughts and feelings have changed. The specialized vocabulary for the critical discussion of drama should provide new ways of looking at plays. But these terms should never be used as devices to limit students or to lock in their exploration to a certain set pattern.

Many students will already be familiar with the main elements of drama, and you may, therefore, want to use this chapter as a review. A light-hearted, yet valid, way to discuss plot, character, dialogue, setting, thought, and so on, is to have students apply these terms to television programs or films with which they are all familiar. For instance, they might consider the importance of setting to programs with similar themes. *M*A*S*H* and *China Beach*, for example, both show a group of Americans facing war in a foreign country. Yet many of each program's episodes are dependent on the specific time and place in which they are set. The political attitudes of the 1960s and 1970s that affect the conflicts in *China Beach* are very different from those of the 1950s that dictate the action in *M*A*S*H*. In addition, the jungles of Vietnam present different hazards from those of the frozen countryside of the Korean winter. Setting, then, is a prominent element in both programs, and it would certainly call for attention if one were writing an analysis or evaluation of the two shows. On the other hand, a program like *Columbo* could easily take place in nearly any large American city, and the program's recent revival suggests that the specific time frame is not highly significant either. *Columbo*, however, provides a wonderful opportunity to look at variations of plot structure. In an intriguing reversal of traditional plot structure, we are shown both the crime and the criminal early on in each episode. We are not carried along by the traditional question, "Who dun it?" but rather by a delicious desire to see how the down-to-earth detective will bring one more wealthy and powerful criminal to his or her knees. With each element, students can offer their own examples and analyses, thus building a bridge between a genre with which they all are familiar (the television program) and drama intended to be performed on the stage (a genre with which they are probably somewhat less familiar).

Plot and Structure

In addition to the main elements of plot and structure explained in the pupil text, you may also want to introduce students to the concept of *subplots*. Whereas most short plays, like *The Rising of the Moon*, present a single, unified action, longer plays often depict a primary action and one or more secondary actions that in some way relate to the main plot. For example, in Tennessee Williams's *The Glass Menagerie*, the main plot focuses on Laura and her struggle to find love and connection in a world from which she becomes increasingly isolated. There are, however, at least two important subplots. One is the story of Amanda, Laura's mother, which is told through her nostalgic, although often painful, memories. The other is Laura's brother Tom's struggle both with his family and with his need to escape his suffocating job. Amanda's and Tom's stories relate to Laura's conflict and its final resolution; the playgoer or reader who gives attention only to Laura's problems misses a great deal of the richness this drama offers.

Students should also be encouraged to watch for variations in plot structure. For instance, a playwright may choose to present actions out of chronological order. In Susan Glaspell's *Trifles*, for example, the story of the Wrights is developed in a scattered fashion, suggesting perhaps the confusion in Minnie's mind as she endured day by day in a cold, emotionally dead marriage. We do not see first the conflict between the Wrights, then John's unspeakably cruel action followed by Minnie's desperate act of revenge, the Sheriff's investigation, and finally the discovery of Minnie's motive. Instead, the story develops through the discoveries and observations of Mrs. Hale and Mrs. Peters, whose unwitting detective work provides an ironic counterpoint to the pompous searching and inquiry of the Sheriff and his men. The women piece together Minnie's story, just as she might have done her quilt. This plot structure allows us to see the developing relationship of the two women both with each other and with their jailed cohort in the sisterhood of women. Understanding the usual pattern of dramatic structure and watching for variations help students to identify key themes and important relationships among characters.

Most carefully constructed plays include *foreshadowing* (clues or suggestions of what will happen later). In fact, a playwright who wants the audience to accept the plausibility of a drama's resolution will certainly provide such hints so that the reader or viewer, coming to the final curtain, will say, "Yes, I can see that now! That's just it! That's the way it would all work out." If the audience has not been prepared, they are likely to come away from the play mystified and unsatisfied. For example, *Macbeth* is filled with portents of what is to come. From the witches' prophecies to Lady Macbeth's sleep-walking revelations, we see a pattern developing that will lead to Macbeth's downfall. As students become adept at noticing foreshadowing, they will enjoy predicting the fortunes of various characters as well as the turns of plot that will seal their fate or lead them to triumph.

Character and Conflict

Just as dramas often have both primary and secondary plots, so do they often have primary and secondary characters who are closely related to each other. These secondary characters, called *foil characters*, reflect in some way the qualities of the primary characters. Whereas foils may share characteristics with protagonists or antagonists, most often they contrast with the main characters. For example, in *Antigonê*, Ismenê provides a foil to Antigonê, and Haimon serves the same function with Creon. Ismenê and Haimon both offer the reasoned, politic course of action and present arguments to their counterparts for choosing the path of compromise. Ismenê, for instance, accepts the limitations society places on females. In the Prologue, she says, "We are only women,/ We cannot fight with men, Antigonê!" (lines 46–47) Ismenê's fears and hesitations underline and emphasize Antigonê's rejection of a subservient role. Unlike Ismenê, Antigonê refuses to yield not only to men, but to anyone who holds earthly power and authority, recognizing only the law of the gods, who decree that the dead must be decently buried. In like manner, Haimon urges his father to be cautious and to listen to reason before he orders Antigonê's death: "You are not in a position to know everything/That people say or do, or what they feel:/Your temper terrifies—everyone/Will tell you only what you like to hear." (Scene III, lines 57–60) Yet Creon, in contrast to this humane and sensible approach, insists on the extreme view, seeing Antigonê as an anarchist and thus a great threat to the power he considers most important, the State. Because the audience hears Haimon's eloquent plea for balance and common sense, Creon's insistence on revenge is underlined as both cruel and irrational.

A useful way to explore characterization is to identify the *conflicts* each individual faces and to define the choices each must make. For example, in *A Raisin in the Sun,* Beneatha's interest in African culture (and particularly her impassioned African dance) provokes conflict with her family, who are uneasy with a background they have sought to escape. Here, then, is an external conflict among the members of the family as well as an internal conflict experienced by Beneatha, who must decide whether to please her family or herself (and her African boyfriend, Asagai). These conflicts are complex and suggest, of course, a larger conflict between the values of white society and the values of a distinct, black culture. There are, of course, other conflicts and other choices in this play: Lena's decision about how to spend the money from Big Walter's insurance; Karl Lindner's choice to try to maintain a segregationist's white Eden; Walter Lee's question about how to earn a living. Each character faces several options or possibilities; each faces controversy and opposition.

Nearly all characters (and certainly every main character) in drama experience conflict. Thoughtful readers and viewers learn to identify these conflicts by asking themselves questions. Are the characters struggling strictly within themselves or primarily against other characters? Are they struggling against an individual or a group? Against a standard, custom, or law established by society? Against a moral law established by religious or ethical principles? Against a natural force (fire, disease)? Students should examine their responses to these conflicts. Are any characters facing choices similar to those students themselves have made (or have watched family and friends make)? And what about the resolutions of those conflicts? How satisfactory are they? Would students have made different choices? Why? How would the play (and the characters) have been altered if the conflicts had been faced in another way?

Dialogue and Monologue

To help students distinguish between the soliloquy and the aside, consider the versions of these two devices used by filmmakers. The *soliloquy* shows us what is inside a character's mind, focusing on that character alone. In a film, this process is often accomplished by a voice-over. We see the character, perhaps walking aimlessly or sitting by a window, while we hear his or her words—not spoken aloud, but rather as though coming directly from the character's inner thoughts. The *aside,* on the other hand, is most delightfully illustrated by Woody Allen films, where the character played by Allen looks directly into the camera and informs viewers of a pithy truth apparently not heard by any of the other characters. In modern film, the aside is used most often for comic effect, although in drama (and particularly in sixteenth-, seventeenth-, and eighteenth-century drama) it is employed in both humorous and serious scenes.

As students read plays that are printed in translation, they should be aware of the difficulties of reading dialogue not rendered in the original tongue of the author (and speakers). For instance, in reading Molière or Ibsen, we must remember that, unlike French or Norwegian, modern English has no equivalent for the two forms of "you." The subtleties of who uses the familiar "you" and who the formal "you" are, therefore, lost. This is, perhaps, a minor problem, yet it suggests the difficulty faced by translators. As a long research project, advanced students might read one of the foreign-language plays in two or more translations and then analyze how the drama is changed by the variance in interpreters' readings.

Although Shakespeare did not write in a foreign language, some students may find Elizabethan English difficult to read. Two approaches have been successful for many teachers and their classes. You might consider giving students a brief summary outline of the play's action (provided on pages 42–45 of this guide). When readers are not struggling to discover who did what to whom, they can pay more attention to what is, after all, the entrancing part of Shakespearean plays—their language. Freeing students from the need to ferret out plot events makes sense from a pedagogical point of view when we stop to remember that Shakespeare rarely created original stories. To some extent then, the student who approaches *Macbeth* already knowing the basic action comes to this drama just as Shakespeare did himself.

The second approach that helps students to become comfortable with the dialogue is to play a tape of parts of the drama—perhaps a scene with the witches or some of the famous soliloquies—several times, stopping for discussion between each repeated playing. Students need to hear the rhythm and cadence of Shakespearean English so that they can duplicate that rhythm and cadence as they read the rest of *Macbeth* (and, of course, other Shakespearean plays) to themselves. As they become confident, they might be asked to prepare readings of scenes themselves.

A final suggestion for working with Shakespearean dialogue and monologue: Consider asking students to memorize at least one significant passage. Although memorization has gone out of style in recent years, perhaps it is time for a reappraisal of this teaching pattern. Certainly forcing students to memorize blindly, with no thought for understanding or interpreting, is hard to defend. We can, however, in good conscience ask students to select ten lines (or twenty) from *Macbeth,* memorize them, present them to the class, and then explain why those lines were chosen. By learning the lines, students internalize the speech patterns of Shakespeare's characters. And often, quite magically, this intense familiarity encourages pleasure and a sense of connection; there is a reason why we call memorizing "learning by heart."

Setting and Staging

As you introduce students to the importance of setting and staging, you may want to mention the changing styles of the theaters for which playwrights created their dramas. The section titled "Genre and Convention" in the pupil text describes and explains in detail the theaters where dramas such as *Antigonê, Macbeth,* and *The Doctor in Spite of Himself* would have been performed. Students should also think about the staging of plays they have seen or in which they have acted. Modern theater has developed many variations, including theater-in-the-round and plays which require actors to mingle with the audience, making the entire building (including the aisles, the lobbies, and even the chairs in which the audience sits) part of the setting. As part of their consideration of modern innovation, students might focus on plays such as Tennessee Williams's *The Glass Menagerie,* where elaborate multimedia staging devices serve to introduce symbols and to reflect the play's themes visually. Williams was one of the first playwrights to combine media, using slides projected onto giant screens to reinforce the action on stage. Twentieth-century stage innovations also include the creative alteration of sets and costumes. For example, a Shakespearean play may be performed in modern dress and with staging that suggests a twentieth-century encampment rather than a medieval fortification. Students may enjoy suggesting such revisionist presentations and should, of course, discuss how the meaning of the play would be changed by such altered sets and costumes.

Symbolism and Irony

When you teach symbolism, you may want to discuss with your students the difference between fixed symbols—such as an eagle symbolizing the United States—and a symbol that takes on a particular meaning within the context of a play. Some symbols, of course, bring their outside, or fixed, associations to plays as well as taking on a meaning within the play, thus creating yet another layer of meaning. Careful thought and evaluation will tell which associations make sense and which do not. For instance, in *The Rising of the Moon,* the moon clearly has symbolic value. If we think of meanings commonly associated with the moon, however, we might come up with something like "romance, magic, mystery." While mystery might apply, certainly romance does not. The moon takes on quite a different significance to the Sergeant and the ballad-singer. The symbolic value, then, must come from within the context of the play.

Irony is a topic that requires careful attention. Most students either know or can easily learn the definitions of the various kinds of irony, and they can understand examples of irony which are carefully labeled and explained. Learning how to detect irony on their own, however, is not so simple. Often inexperienced readers will take as literal dialogue, situations, or characterizations that a more experienced reader will easily recognize as ironic. As you teach each play, watch for examples of irony and suggest to students the cues that let readers/viewers know a playwright is being ironic. For example, repeated phrases and exaggerated actions often indicate irony. Consider *An Enemy of the People,* where the title phrase is repeated frequently, often in a dramatic and inflammatory manner. The irony, of course, lies in the fact that those who cast the accusation most readily at the Doctor show themselves likely candidates for the title they use to label him. Both the repetition of the phrase and the circumstances under which it is delivered are clues to Ibsen's irony.

You might bring to class—or invite students to bring to class—examples of verbal and visual irony. They may also enjoy giving examples of irony they have seen on television programs or in films. Becoming sensitive to irony is a gradual process and one that seems to need much cautious encouragement. No one likes to feel that she or he did not "get the joke," so you may want to avoid a guessing-game approach and concentrate instead on group analysis where students freely offer their interpretations of ironic cartoons, articles, books, and so on.

Thought and Theme

The most important point to emphasize in teaching "Thought and Theme" is the recursive nature of the reading/viewing experience. As we watch or read a play, we have certain emotional and intellectual responses. Later, thinking about the drama, we may modify, reaffirm, or entirely reject those initial responses. Plays, in general, do not yield one unchanging "true" meaning, but instead offer a wealth of possibilities.

To emphasize the evolving nature of reading/viewing, ask the students to consider a play they saw as children (perhaps *Peter Pan*). If they saw no plays as children, they almost certainly saw children's films (again *Peter Pan* would work well). Have them try to recreate what they felt and thought when they first saw the play and then compare that with what they think or feel now when they reconsider it. For instance, how does Peter's desire to stay a boy, to "never grow up," strike them? And how about Peter's bringing Wendy back to Never-Never Land to serve as a mother for the lost boys (a role that includes primarily cooking and sewing for them)? As students discuss their changing responses, they will see how any play, and certainly those that are far more complex than *Peter Pan*, offers multiple themes that grow and develop with each rereading or re-viewing.

Genre and Convention

You may want to assign this section as an introduction to genre and convention at the beginning of the study of drama. You might also consider reassigning certain parts as you teach individual plays. These are possibilities:

Antigonê	Tragedy (pages 50–51) Greek Drama (pages 53–54)
The Tragedy of Macbeth	Tragedy (pages 50–51) Elizabethan Drama (pages 54–55)
The Doctor in Spite of Himself	Comedy (pages 51–52) Neoclassical Drama (pages 55–56)
An Enemy of the People	Tragicomedy (page 52) Modern Realistic and Absurdist Drama (pages 56–57)
A Marriage Proposal	Comedy (pages 51–52)
The Gap	Modern Realistic and Absurdist Drama (pages 56–57)
True West	Modern Realistic and Absurdist Drama (pages 56–57)

In addition to thinking about the differences between various genres and between the dramatic conventions of different eras, students should also notice the distinctions between one-act plays and longer plays. In some ways, those distinctions are similar to the differences between short stories and novels. The shorter works usually take place in one setting, depict one main action, and include only a few characters. Longer plays often change settings, depict several actions (including subplots and parallel plots), and include more characters. These generalizations, of course, do not always hold true. Some longer plays, for instance, focus primarily on the conflicts of only one or two main characters. Still, it is worthwhile for students to consider why a playwright has chosen a particular length to examine particular themes and to imagine how the play might have changed had it been shorter or longer.

PART TWO

About the Plays

Antigonê

Sophocles (496?–406 B.C.)

A handsome soldier and politician, Sophocles was also a priest and a tragic dramatist. He was born at Colonus in Attica and as a youth was chosen to lead the chorus at major festivals because of his physical beauty and grace of performance. Following Aeschylus as the favored writer of Greek drama, Sophocles won a stunning victory in 468 B.C. in the traditional Athenian Spring Drama competition. The tragedy submitted by Aeschylus was defeated by a tragedy Sophocles had written. This triumph occurred when Sophocles was only 28 years old, and his winning was attributed at least in part to his innovative approach. In Aeschylus' tragedies, only two actors appeared on the stage at the same time, but Sophocles introduced a third. He went on to write more than 120 plays, 20 of which gained the first prize and none of which earned less than second. Although about a thousand fragments of various plays remain, only seven have survived as complete works. These include *Ajax, Antigonê, Oedipus Rex, Electra, Philoctetes, The Trachinian Women,* and *Oedipus at Colonus.*

Sophocles lived to be almost 100 years old and, during his lifetime, saw the Greeks rise to power over the Persian Empire. The statesman Pericles, who made peace with Sparta and ruled during Athens' Golden Age (461–429 B.C.), greatly admired Sophocles and favored his work. Toward the end of Sophocles' life, the power of Athens declined, partly a result of the energy and expense drained by the Peloponnesian War. Sophocles, however, maintained his creative genius until the end of his life, and his final play, *Oedipus at Colonus,* was written when he was nearly 90. It is an amazing tribute to him that two of his plays, *Oedipus Rex* and *Antigonê,* are still regularly performed and evoke the pity, terror, and admiration of audiences today just as they did in ancient Athens.

Greek Drama

Because Greek drama is so different from what most modern viewers and readers expect, students need to understand that it evolved from religious rituals. Several excellent films and slide-tapes are available to illustrate the structure of the Greek amphitheater and the formal and rigid nature of the costumes and masks. As students visualize the physical location and appearance of the actors, they will come to appreciate the way this physical formality is balanced by equally formal, structured language.

The structure of Greek drama is very different from the standard acts and scenes of contemporary drama or even of Shakespearean drama. Students may find it helpful to review this structure before reading *Antigonê*. Sophocles' tragedies open with a *prologue* that establishes the conflict, followed by a *párodos,* a song the chorus sings as it enters the stage. The play progresses in a series of *scenes,* each of which builds, or later resolves, the conflict. Each scene is followed by an *ode* that presents the communal voice of the chorus. The play ends with an *exodos* that concludes the action.

The characters in Greek tragedy play stylized roles. Their masks and costumes help to create universal characters rather than individual people, which may make it difficult for students to relate to them. This distance is reinforced because the characters and plots are derived from myths well known to the Greek audiences. On the other hand, students usually relate well to the conflict in Sophocles' tragedies. Although he presents us with situations that occurred centuries ago, the issues raised are still relevant. Sophocles sees human beings in conflict with the world around them. His characters experience not only internal conflicts, but also conflicts with society, government control, laws and customs, nature, gods, and a sense of justice.

Greek drama has strongly influenced Western theater. Modern tragic characters are still examined for characteristics that fall into the patterns established in Aristotle's *Poetics,* based on his first-hand observation of drama. Students who understand Greek drama not only know more about our heritage—the myths and the rituals, the poetry and the music—but they also are better able to appreciate the evolution of drama from the seventeenth through the twentieth centuries presented in this text.

Teaching the Play

Students will be able to understand the play more fully if they understand the background of Polyneicês' death. Few students will have read *Oedipus Rex*, although they may be familiar with parts of the story. They should, therefore, pay special attention to the footnote on student text page 61 to prepare them for the tragedy of the family history that Ismenê summarizes in lines 36–42 of the prologue. Oedipus, following his discovery of his incestuous marriage to his mother, exiled himself from Thebes, and his two sons, Eteoclês and Polyneicês, became the ruling monarchs. Although they originally agreed to reign in alternate years, Eteoclês (who was the first to assume the throne) refused to step down when his allotted time had passed. Polyneicês convinced Adrastus, the king of Argos, to join with him to remove Eteoclês forcibly. As a result of the attack on Thebes, Polyneicês and Eteoclês engaged in a duel and killed each other. Creon (the brother of Iocastê, Oedipus's mother and wife) assumed the throne and declared that Eteoclês should be buried with full honors. Because Polyneicês had committed the sin of attacking his native city, his body was to be shamed by lying in the field where he fell.

The following chart clarifies the relationships among the Theban royal families:

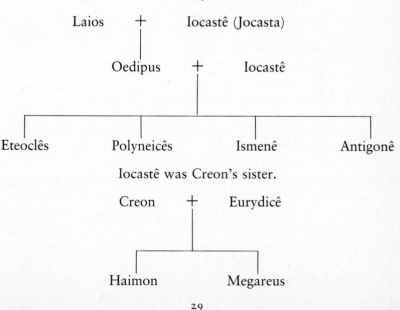

Labdacus, grandson of Kadmos, founder
of Thebes, father of Laios

Laios   +   Iocastê (Jocasta)

Oedipus   +   Iocastê

Eteoclês   Polyneicês   Ismenê   Antigonê

Iocastê was Creon's sister.

Creon   +   Eurydicê

Haimon   Megareus

The stage directions for *Antigonê* are simple, stating that the play begins at dawn in front of the palace in Thebes. Antigonê and Ismenê enter from the palace, engaged in a conversation that clearly establishes their relationship and the conflicts between them: Antigonê and Ismenê disagree about burying their brother, Polyneicês, and about the necessity to uphold Creon's edict forbidding the burial.

The tension builds slowly; Antigonê and Creon do not come face to face until Scene II. The clash between law (as defined by Creon) and justice (as advocated by Antigonê) forms one of the play's primary themes. As with other Greek tragedies, each scene focuses on a specific theme-related issue that emerges through the confrontation of two characters (with a third actor often commenting or interjecting additional information).

Summary of Antigonê

The structure of *Antigonê* follows the traditional format of a Greek tragedy:

Prologue Antigonê informs her sister Ismenê of Creon's edict not to bury their brother Polyneicês and of her decision to bury him despite the threat of death. Ismenê refuses to help, citing women's roles, reluctance to defy the law, and concern for public good as her reasons. Antigonê is determined to bury her brother, regardless of the consequences.

Párodos The chorus and the Choragos tell of the great battle in which Polyneicês, leader of the attacking army, and his brother Eteoclês, loyal defender of Thebes, killed each other "[f]ace to face in matchless rage."

Scene I Creon, as the new king of Thebes, announces his values to the chorus, followed by his public proclamation not to bury Polyneicês. A sentry who had been guarding the body of Polyneicês enters, terrified, to tell Creon that someone had mounded "[n]ew dust on the slimy flesh!" Creon is irate, perhaps even paranoid, first questioning the guard and then arguing with the Choragos. The bold sentry leaves, swearing never to return.

Ode I The chorus offers a philosophical comment in Strophe 1: "Numberless are the world's wonders, but none/More wonderful than man . . ."; Antistrophe 1 comments that man is more powerful than wild animals. Strophe 2 notes that man "has made himself secure—from all but . . . death . . . "; Antistrophe 2 praises intelligence, which works to keep the law.

Scene II The sentry brings in Antigonê, accusing her of burying Polyneicês. When he tells Creon the story, Antigonê says, "I deny nothing." She says she prefers death to living in a corrupt society. After the Choragos reminds us of her father (Oedipus), Creon and Antigonê argue about the honoring of the dead. Creon decides to involve Ismenê, who now wants some credit for the burial; Antigonê refuses. Creon orders both Antigonê and Ismenê taken away.

Ode II Strophe 1 alludes to the tragedy of Oedipus, and Antistrophe 1 comments on its impact on Oedipus's children. Strophe 2 refers to the arrogance of Creon: "No pride on earth is free of the curse of heaven"; Antistrophe 2 warns the audience that "[m]an's little pleasure is the spring of sorrow."

Scene III Haimon, Creon's son and Antigonê's fiancé, vows love and support for Creon, who says Haimon will be better off without Antigonê. Haimon suggests that Creon be flexible and seek the opinions of others. Creon argues that "[t]he State is the King!" Once Haimon realizes that Creon is blind to reason, he leaves. Despite a warning from the Choragos, Creon orders Antigonê's death.

Ode III The Strophe warns of the power of love; the Antistrophe warns that no one benefits from the love we see here.

Scene IV The Choragos mourns Antigonê's impending death. In Strophe 1, Antigonê says good-bye; the chorus speaks of her honor. In Antistrophe 1, Antigonê recalls the story of Niobê, who was turned into stone; the chorus responds that, unlike Niobê, Antigonê is mortal. In Strophe 2, Antigonê worries that she is laughed at and "[u]njustly judged"; the chorus wonders what role Oedipus' fate plays in Antigonê's death. In Antistrophe 2, Antigonê castigates Oedipus, "father and brother" for the "blasphemy of my birth"; the chorus responds that "[y]our death is the doing of your conscious hand." In the Epode, Antigonê pleads for death. When Creon orders her taken away, Antigonê welcomes her death.

Ode IV The chorus comments that "[n]o power . . . [c]an prevail against untiring Destiny," recalling gruesome tales of those who had argued and defied the gods.

Scene V Teiresias, an old wise man, describes some recent disturbances of nature and states that Creon himself has "brought/ This new calamity upon us." Even when Teiresias warns that "[t]he only crime is pride," Creon responds that "[n]o man can defile the gods," and refuses to change his sentence upon Antigonê. Only when the Choragos reminds Creon that Teiresias has never been wrong does Creon decide to free Antigonê.

Paean The interplay between the chorus and the Choragos calls upon Iacchos (Bacchos, or Dionysos, god of wine and revelry).

Exodos A messenger describes the change in Creon, from "happy once" to "a walking dead man." The messenger reports to the Choragos the deaths of Haimon and Antigonê. Eurydicê, wife of Creon and mother of Haimon, enters the scene for the first time. The messenger tells her of going with Creon to give honorable burial to the body of Polyneicês and of their finding the bodies of Haimon and Antigonê. Eurydicê enters the palace and commits suicide. Creon realizes, too late, that "[m]y own blind heart has brought me/From darkness to final darkness." The Choragos concludes the play saying, ". . . proud men in old age learn to be wise."

Discussion and Writing Topics

1. *Describe the central conflict of the play. Whose rights should assume priority—Creon's to legislate and punish, or Antigonê's to bury her brother? Is there any way to resolve the competing claims of Creon and Antigonê?*

Students should understand that Creon, new king of Thebes, has forbidden the burial of his nephew Polyneicês as punishment for attacking the city. The central conflict of the play arises when Antigonê, Polyneicês' sister, declares her intention to bury her brother. She argues that to do otherwise would dishonor the gods. (Students will understand the depth of Antigonê's feelings when they know that, according to Greek religious beliefs, the soul of a person who had not received proper burial could not take its proper place in the underworld.) Creon, of course, insists on the importance of the state and of avoiding anarchy through enforcing the dictates of the state.

After they understand the central problem, students will probably argue vehemently about whether Creon or Antigonê has the stronger case. Both have a legitimate position: Creon has social and political laws to uphold; Antigonê has honor and religious obligations to fulfill. But both also step beyond their roles: Creon oversteps his authority in his lack of reverence for the gods, and Antigonê is perhaps too willing to be a martyr.

As discussion evolves, you may want to introduce the position described by the literary scholar Charles Paul Segal in his essay "Sophocles' Praise of Man and the Conflicts of the *Antigonê*":

> We must avoid seeing the protagonists as one-dimensional representatives of simple oppositions: right and wrong, reason and emotion, state and individual, or the like. Such oppositions have some validity, but a validity purchased at the price of oversimplification and ultimately a misunderstanding of Sophocles' sense of the tragic.

Segal goes on to say that the characters and their issues require a more complex response than simply deciding who is right:

> Recent critics, abandoning the simple thesis-antithesis opposition and looking at the play in terms of the action itself, have made it clear that it is hard to find much pure "right" on Creon's side, though this is not to say that his fate entirely lacks a tragic dimension or that the conflict is settled merely by a kind of moral default. Antigonê, on the other hand, is vindicated by the end of the play, but only at the cost of tremendous suffering, her own and that of those closest to her.

2. What is Haimon's role in the play? What does Haimon's dialogue with his father reveal about the two characters?

Haimon parallels Antigonê's decision to demonstrate that beliefs are worth dying for. Of all the characters, Haimon comes closest to understanding Antigonê's decision. On the other hand, Haimon also acts as a foil to his father, Creon, when he tries to convince his father to balance justice with mercy. Haimon does not see the world in political absolutes as does his father. Despite Haimon's youth (Creon refers to him as an "adolescent fool"), he demonstrates insight into his father's nature. His ability to act as a wise and honorable diplomat in Scene III suggests that he would have made a fine ruler. He knows that Creon will be pleased if he "subordinate[s]/Everything . . . to [his] father's will," so he begins gently. He suggests that "[r]eason is God's crowning gift to man," urging Creon to consider that others' "opinions might be helpful." When Creon is not persuaded, Haimon strengthens his argument:

> They say no woman has ever, so unreasonably,
> Died so shameful a death for a generous act:

Creon apparently remains unmoved, so Haimon reminds Creon that he has "no right to trample on God's right." Haimon and Creon clearly disagree about what is "just." Haimon's sense of justice is much broader than Creon's and moves beyond what the rigid monarch can understand until his terrible, tragic insight at the end of the play.

3. What do Ismenê and Euridycê contribute to the play? How would Antigonê *differ if either or both were absent?*

Both Ismenê and Antigonê share the desire to see their brother buried. Antigonê shows herself as the stronger of the two almost immediately when she proposes the defiant act of interring Polyneicês' body. Ismenê then becomes a foil for Antigonê by providing a vivid contrast. While Antigonê is bold, decisive, and defiant, Ismenê is timid, indecisive, and submissive. Antigonê has a strong sense of justice; Ismenê is more concerned with propriety. Antigonê is absolute in her sense of "right"; Ismenê is swayed by the views of other people and by the circumstances in which she finds herself. Students will note, however, that Ismenê is not, in the final analysis, a coward. When Creon sentences Antigonê to death, Ismenê declares her intention to die with her sister. She goes as far as confessing to having collaborated with Antigonê on the burial when, in fact, she had not. If Ismenê were not in the play, we would fail to see many of the complexities of both the central conflict and the character of Antigonê.

Eurydicê, by her suicide, emphasizes the impact of Creon's decision, his unwillingness to listen to reason. She also contributes to the play by partially fulfilling Teiresias' prophecy.

4. *Considering the emphasis in the play on Creon, why isn't the play titled* Creon *instead of* Antigonê? *Who is the tragic hero, Creon or Antigonê? Use the definition of tragic hero provided in the student text (p. 50).*

Some critics have seen Creon as such an important character in the play that they have argued that the title should bear his name rather than Antigonê's. Students often find this an interesting point to discuss and usually decide that although Creon may, in fact, fulfill the criteria of tragic hero, the play is correctly titled because Antigonê is the one who sacrifices her life for her principles and values. Although she is obsessed and dies for her beliefs, she exposes social injustice and shows how people may extend themselves beyond normal limits.

5. *How does Sophocles use speeches, actions, and gestures to characterize Creon and Antigonê? Give examples to support your answer.*

Creon's long, often angry, speeches (Scene III, for example) and his sweeping entries (Scene I) suggest his strong, stubborn adherence to his role as ruler. Antigonê, also stubborn, demonstrates through her direct, absolute statements and her offstage actions when she buries her brother that she adheres to uncompromising values.

There are few stage directions given, but students will notice that Creon frequently speaks "furiously" or is "completely out of control"; Antigonê, on the other hand, is never described in such negative terms, thus slanting audience sympathy toward her rather than toward the king.

6. *Describe the structure of the play. How is its plot constructed and developed? Where does the climax ocur? How do the poetic odes that punctuate the play affect its dramatic action?*

A detailed summary of the structure is provided on pages 30–32 of this guide. The climax of the play (the point of its greatest tension) occurs in Scene III when Creon becomes increasingly incensed with Haimon and sentences Antigonê to death. The poetic odes slow down the action and provide a commentary on the play's themes; these odes allow the audience to contemplate what they have seen before they move on to the next action.

7. *What is the role of the chorus? Single out two important comments made by the chorus and explain their significance.*

The chorus comments on the action, both with philosophical observations and with attempts to sway the characters. Students might select one of these comments:

Ode I honors the power of man, safe from everything but death.

Ode II reminds the audience of the fate of Oedipus and his children and of the imminent downfall of Creon because of pride.

Scene IV, Antistrophe 2, reminds Antigonê that her death is directly the result of her "conscious hand."

The Choragos, considered as a separate voice from the chorus, is even more important to the play. The following scenes might be analyzed:

Scene I: The Choragos agrees to support Creon (line 50). Later in the scene the Choragos questions if the gods might have buried Polyneicês (line 104).

Scene III: The Choragos notes that Haimon makes good sense (lines 92–93). Later in the same scene, the Choragos warns Creon that Haimon's rage is dangerous (line 135).

8. *Select an engaging scene and explain how you would stage it. Consider the scenery, lighting, costumes, and the positions and gestures of the actors. You may use what you have learned about Greek theater, or you may choose to include some modern touches.*

Responses will vary, of course. Students should choose a scene that works as a unit of meaning (for example, the conversation in the prologue between Ismenê and Antigonê or the confrontation between Antigonê and Creon in Scene II, beginning with line 50 and ending with line 120).

Going Further

1. Compare Antigonê's tragedy with Creon's suffering. Which character do you sympathize with most? Why?

2. Do you consider Antigonê a fanatic, desperate to martyr herself, or a rational person whose beliefs are so strong that she is willing to risk civil disobedience?

3. Investigate the beliefs and attitudes of Greek citizens in the fifth century B.C. Would the original audience have been more in sympathy with Creon or Antigonê?

4. Read Oedipus Rex and compare Oedipus and Creon. Do you agree, as some scholars have argued, that Oedipus is the better ruler in spite of his flaws and Creon the poorer ruler in spite of his virtues? Explain your view.

5. Read Jean Anouilh's Antigonê, and compare the differences between Anouilh's and Sophocles' versions. Explain whether you agree or disagree with the changes that Anouilh has made. Has he tampered with the story too much? Has he legitimately updated it for twentieth-century audiences? If you were to update the story for today's readers and viewers, what changes would you make?

The Tragedy of Macbeth

William Shakespeare (1564–1616)

Of all the playwrights represented in *Reading Drama*, Shakespeare is most likely to be familiar to students. Some will have read his poems and at least one of his plays. All will recognize his name.

Many will know the names of his more famous characters, quotations from well-known speeches, and tidbits of biography. You might begin by asking students what they know about Shakespeare and proceeding from their observations.

Some students may have heard that Shakespeare never really existed and that his plays were actually written by someone else (perhaps Sir Walter Raleigh or even Queen Elizabeth I herself). Careful research, however, establishes that a person named William Shakespeare did, in fact, live, write, and act in plays. While there is no birth certificate, for example, church records show that he was baptized on Wednesday, April 26, 1564. His father, John, was a prosperous merchant who dealt primarily in gloves as well as other leather goods and in grain. In addition, John Shakespeare served as a town official. His mother, Mary, was the daughter of a wealthy farmer who apparently married "down," as she lost her right to her father's coat of arms when she wed John before he officially became a "gentleman."

While we have little direct evidence concerning Shakespeare's childhood, he almost certainly entered the grammar school of his native Stratford-on-Avon, where he would have been entitled to free education. When he was about 12 years old, however, his father suffered grave financial losses, and it is probable that William was removed from school to join the family business. A neighbor, noting his early talent for words, is quoted as saying, "When he kill'd a calf, he would doe it in a high style and make a speech." Although he may have left school early and although, as Ben Jonson observed, "he had but little Latine and lesse Greek," tradition has it that Shakespeare served as a country schoolmaster in his youth.

A bond dated November 28, 1582, authenticates his marriage to Anne Hathaway, who (according to the inscription on her tombstone) was eight years older than her 18-year-old groom. On May 26, 1583, Anne and William Shakespeare's first child, Susanna, was baptized, followed in February 1585 by the baptism of their twin son and daughter, Hamnet and Judith. Sometime after the arrival of the children, Shakespeare left Stratford-on-Avon for London. The reasons for his departure are not certain, although one tradition has it that he indulged in deer poaching, was caught, and subsequently wrote scandalous verses about the gentleman who prosecuted him. The aftermath of this series of events supposedly encouraged one of literary history's most fortunate migrations. Whether or not this anecdote is completely accurate, the fact remains that by 1592 William Shakespeare had established himself in London as an actor and had begun to write plays. Students interested in Shakespeare as a participant in drama might read Hamlet's advice to the players (*Hamlet*, Act II, Scene II) to see how carefully Shakespeare had considered not only what a playwright creates but also how the actors deliver that creation to the audience. Although Shakespeare was described as an excellent actor by many contemporary critics, he was attacked by playwright Robert Greene in *Groatsworth of Wit* for daring to step from the stage to take up the pen. Greene called Shakespeare "an upstart Crow" who "supposes he is as well able to bombast out a blanke verse as the best of you" (the currently ranking dramatists).

In 1594 Shakespeare performed at court for Queen Elizabeth and he steadily gained both in reputation and in wealth. His name was associated with the prestigious Burbage's theater company, and in 1599 he is listed as one of the owners of the Globe Theater. By this time he had been granted his own coat of arms and had had his mother's coat of arms restored; thus he was officially recognized not only as an outstanding dramatist but also as a "gentleman." When James I ascended to the throne, Shakespeare remained a favorite, and he and his company were ceremoniously dubbed the "King's Men" in May 1603. Shakespeare continued his prolific writing of dramas, but it is doubtful that he acted after he and his company purchased the Blackfriars Theater in 1609, using this as their winter quarters when inclement weather prevented production at the Globe.

Shakespeare died on April 23, 1616, leaving substantial bequests to his family and friends, including, of course, the famous "second-best bed" which he designated to his wife. Since Anne Shakespeare was already entitled, as a widow, to a third of the income of the estate as well as tenancy in the family home, this much-discussed bequest does not necessarily indicate stormy weather in the Shakespeare marriage. Following the playwright's burial, a stone was laid over his grave with the memorable inscription (supposedly dictated by the bard) which has fascinated generations of scholars and tourists alike:

Good Frend for Jesus Sake Forbeare
To Digg the Dust Enclosed Heare!
Bleste Be Ye Man Yt Spares Thes Stones
And Curst Be He Yt Moves My Bones.

The Elizabethan Theater

Although students often find the drama of ancient Greece unfamiliar in style and structure, most have read at least one or two Shakespearean plays. Yet, despite their previous experience—or perhaps because of it—they are often filled with apprehension about their ability to understand Elizabethan language.

Classroom discussion that establishes useful background material helps put students at ease. Many students have some knowledge of the Globe Theater (see student text, pp. 54–55) and the social and political realities of sixteenth- and seventeenth-century England, so this may be a good place to begin. Students should know, for instance, that Henry VIII (and his six unfortunate wives) held the throne of England from 1509 to 1547 and that Henry was succeeded by Edward VI, Mary, and then by Henry the VIII's daughter, Elizabeth I, whose name the age of Shakespeare bears. During Elizabeth's reign (1558–1603) Galileo was born and Michelangelo died (in the same year, 1564). Sir Francis Drake, whose fortunes waxed and waned in Elizabeth's court, distinguished himself by circling the globe in 1580. In 1588 the Spanish Armada was defeated, and four years after Elizabeth's death a stalwart group of English men and women sailed for the New World and established the Jamestown Colony in what is now Virginia.

In discussing the possibilities and limitations of Elizabethan theaters, students may be interested to know that drama troops, playwrights, and directors of that period had intricate sets and apparatus at their disposal. For instance, at the theater where Shakespeare first performed, five different levels were available, beginning with trapdoors in the stage floor, which allowed creatures from the netherworld to spring up suddenly, surprising both the characters on the main stage as well as the audience. The main stage had a central area, a jutting front (for large actions, such as battles), and a small inner platform to serve as a private room or other interior space. As anyone who has read or seen *Romeo and*

Juliet might imagine, the theater also offered a balcony, and even higher up, under the roof, were a number of machines that allowed gods, birds, stars, and other heavenly or flying objects to be introduced when called for. Drama flourished during this era and no expense was spared to create illusions that alternately entertained, terrified, amused, and amazed the audience.

Shakespeare's plays share a great deal with twentieth-century theater, not only the tremendous amount of action (often violent) and the humor (both subtle and bawdy) but also the in-depth character development and the complex plots.

Teaching the Play

Here is an incredibly modern play, written by an Elizabethan and set in eleventh-century Scotland. Shakespeare's *Macbeth* raises questions about the pressures of ambition, about the nature of a good ruler or leader, about political morality and immorality. These are issues students hear discussed every day in the news media, and they should certainly have opinions about them. You might begin by asking students to define ambition and to explain whether they believe ambition to be an admirable quality. Obviously, this question cannot be answered with a simple yes or no, and students' responses should lead to a discussion of the problems that can arise when a particular ambition becomes an obsession. If time permits, you might also ask the class to define a "good" leader; what qualities would that person have? As they begin to read *Macbeth,* they meet a man who soon burns with the ambition to be king but who has never really considered what it means to be a good leader.

Students should pay particular attention to Macbeth's long asides and soliloquies, as these speeches explain the workings of his mind and conscience from the beginning of his quest for the crown to his downfall and death. In these speeches we learn how Macbeth regards Duncan, how he justifies the murders he plans, how he thinks of Lady Macbeth, and finally what he sees as the meaning (or lack of meaning) in human life. A thought-provoking topic for discussion, warm-up writing, or journal writing: What figures from history—or from today's news reports—face choices similar to Macbeth's? You might encourage students to think not only of political figures but also of people in other professions.

Two enjoyable supplementary teaching resources:

1. *Shakespeare Persona: A Creative Approach to Writing*. Rebecca Carosso and Elizabeth Foster. Littleton, Mass.: Sundance Publishers, 1985. This book provides writing assignments that encourage students to imagine themselves as characters in Shakespeare's plays and to write from within that persona.

2. *Twisted Tales from Shakespeare*. Richard Armour. New York: McGraw-Hill, 1957. Armour offers a series of delightful parodies, including a spoof of *Macbeth*. After students have worked through the play and learned to enjoy Shakespeare, you may want to offer them this lighthearted look at the bard written by a professor of English who is himself an Elizabethan scholar.

Summary of The Tragedy of Macbeth

Act I The three weird sisters, witches, gather in a sinister, storm-filled setting to introduce the action. The action then moves to a battle camp where Duncan, King of Scotland, learns from Ross, a nobleman, of the Norwegian king's defeat. Macbeth, Thane of Glamis, has shown particular bravery, and Duncan rewards him by sentencing to death the traitor Thane of Cawdor and giving Macbeth his title. Before Macbeth receives the news, the weird sisters accost him and proclaim him Thane of Glamis, Thane of Cawdor, and "king hereafter." Banquo, who accompanies Macbeth, is told that he will father kings although he will not be crowned himself. Macbeth is understandably shaken when messengers arrive from Duncan to confirm part of the witches' strange prophecy. At first Macbeth fears his good fortune, but when he discovers that Malcolm, Duncan's son, has been made Prince of Cumberland (and thus successor to the throne), he considers killing Malcolm to eliminate a rival for the crown. When Macbeth returns home to Inverness, Lady Macbeth urges him to kill Duncan, who will visit them that evening. The final scene of Act I shows Macbeth wrestling with his conscience in the famous soliloquy beginning, "If it were done when 'tis done, then 'twere well,/It were done quickly." Interrupting him, Lady Macbeth taunts him with lack of manliness and reveals her plan to fulfill her vow that the king "[m]ust be provided for."

Act II Banquo and his son Fleance, walking that night in the court of Macbeth's castle, come upon Macbeth. Banquo tells Macbeth that he is worried about the witches' prophecies, which he resists aiding. Macbeth brushes off Banquo's concerns and in a soliloquy imagines a bloody dagger before his eyes. Lady Macbeth, according to her plan, has encouraged the grooms in the king's bedchamber to get drunk. Macbeth enters Duncan's bedroom (off-stage) and stabs him with the grooms' daggers. When the body is discovered in the morning, Macbeth and Lady Macbeth feign sorrow and anguish while placing blame on the grooms, whom Macbeth kills, claiming he was overcome by fury when he found them smeared with the king's blood. Malcolm and Donalbain, Duncan's sons, fear that they, too, will be murdered. They decide to flee from Scotland, thus creating suspicion that they were somehow involved in their father's death. Macbeth is crowned at Scone, thus fulfilling the witches' prophecy.

Act III Banquo ponders Macbeth's role in Duncan's death as well as the possibility that the weird sisters' prophecies regarding his own fortunes may come true. When Macbeth learns that Banquo and Fleance plan to take a ride in the afternoon, he hires two murderers (who are later joined by a third) to kill both father and son. Lady Macbeth encourages her husband to appear more cheerful, but he hints at the dark thoughts he holds in his heart. She urges him to tell her more about his plans for Banquo and Fleance, but he declares his intention to keep her innocent of the deed until it is done. The three murderers kill Banquo, but Fleance escapes, bearing in mind his father's final words demanding revenge. In the next scene, Macbeth and Lady Macbeth greet their guests at a banquet. Macbeth begins to praise Banquo, but is stopped by an apparition of the dead man, whom only Macbeth can see. Lady Macbeth covers for her husband's horrified reaction by claiming he suffers from a recurring illness and dismisses the guests. Left alone with his wife, Macbeth expresses his fear that Banquo's death will bring revenge. He vows to seek the weird sisters to discover their further prophecies. In a new scene, Hecate, the witches' leader, scolds the sisters for their relationship with Macbeth and orders them to bring their charms to the next day's meeting. In the final scene we learn that Macduff, another Scottish nobleman, has joined forces with Malcolm, Duncan's son, in England, where they seek help from Siward, the Earl of Northumberland, to defeat Macbeth.

Act IV The witches begin this act, moving quickly into their famous "Double, double, toil and trouble" incantation. Macbeth appears and demands that they answer his questions. In response, they summon a series of ghostly apparitions. The first, an armed head, tells him to beware of Macduff, the Thane of Fife. The second, a bloody child, announces that no man born of woman shall harm Macbeth. The third apparition, a crowned child who holds a tree, declares that Macbeth need have no fear until "Great Birnam Wood to high Dunsinane Hill/Shall come." Finally, in response to Macbeth's asking whether Banquo's descendants will ever reign, the witches summon a line of eight kings who pass by, the last carrying a mirror in which many more kings appear. Banquo's ghost follows these kings, showing that they are his kin. As the witches disappear, Lennox, another nobleman, enters and denies having seen the weird sisters. He informs Macbeth that Macduff has fled to England, and Macbeth vows revenge. In the next scene, Lady Macduff and her young son are talking when a messenger interrupts, warning them to flee. The alarm comes too late, however, and both Lady Macduff and her children are murdered by Macbeth's assassins. Meanwhile, Malcolm and Macduff are in England, where Malcolm tests Macduff's loyalty by declaring that he (Malcolm) will make a much worse king than Macbeth. When Macduff falls into an agony of grief, Malcolm admits he has falsely described himself to make sure of Macduff's beliefs. Ross then enters bearing the horrifying news of the murder of Lady Macduff and her children. Grief stricken, Macduff vows revenge, swearing that he will never rest until he confronts Macbeth.

Act V Act V opens with Lady Macbeth's sleepwalking scene. She imagines her hands to be stained and repeatedly tries to wash away both the spots she thinks she sees and her guilt over the crimes she and Macbeth have committed. Meanwhile, Macbeth, although deeply concerned about his wife's disorder, prepares frantically for the attack of Malcolm, Macduff, and the English invaders who have now joined forces with Scottish rebels under the command of Menteith, Angus, Lennox, and Caithness. Macbeth remains confident he is safe because of the witches' prophecies, but he laments that he rules through power alone and lacks the respect, love, and honor given to a just monarch. Malcolm orders his troops to cut boughs from trees to carry as camouflage as they attack, thus fulfilling the condition that Birnam Wood should come to Dunsinane. Macbeth learns of Malcolm's ploy just after he receives another shock—the news of his wife's death, probably a suicide. He muses about the implications of her death in his soliloquy beginning, "She should have died hereafter. . . ." Macbeth goes into battle, kills Northumberland's son, and then encounters Macduff, who admits that he was born through what modern medicine calls a Caesarean section and is therefore not, technically, "of woman born." With his last apparent protection destroyed, Macbeth is killed by Macduff. Macduff then brings Macbeth's head to Malcolm, and all hail both the death of the traitorous tyrant and Malcolm's ascension to the throne. Order is restored, and the new king appoints as earls the nobles who helped him.

Discussion and Writing Topics

1. *What makes Macbeth a tragic figure? Is his tragedy self-inflicted, or is it something beyond his control? What is his tragic flaw?*

Macbeth is a brave officer who, at the beginning of the play, has just acted courageously to defend king and country against the attacking Norwegian forces. We learn of Macbeth's strength and potential early in the drama, just as we see him as a kind and devoted husband. Lady Macbeth herself characterizes him as "too full o' th' milk of human kindness" (Act I, Scene V, line 15), and Macbeth's agonizing over whether or not to kill the good, and elderly, King Duncan shows that he is certainly not simply a power-hungry villain. Because Macbeth holds a high station in his society and because he has many worthy qualities, his fall should certainly be considered tragic. Although there are forces that apparently impel Macbeth (the weird sisters, pressure from Lady Macbeth), his constant soul-searching throughout the play suggests that he is, in fact, in charge of his own fate. We should note that, above all, Macbeth is an imaginative man. He sees daggers and ghosts, he entertains the prophecies of witches, and he is also able to project the horror of killing each of his victims and to envision the consequences not only to himself but also to the society in which he lives. With such an ability to project alternatives and results, Macbeth seems a figure who must take the major responsibility for his own downfall. His tragic flaw is ambition. In *Shakespeare, Our Contemporary* (Doubleday, 1966), Jan Kott notes, "Ambition means in this play the intention and planning of murder." Kott claims that murder is the primary theme in *Macbeth,* yet surely it is ambition run amok that leads to the initial killing. We need only look at Banquo for a contrast. He is also told by the weird sisters that extraordinary power is possible for his line. Yet he refuses to act immorally in order to speed or ensure the fulfillment of that prophecy.

2. Lady Macbeth is a resourceful and clever character who knows how to manipulate others. Explain how she manipulates Macbeth.

Lady Macbeth knows her husband very well and understands fully his deep devotion to her. While she lacks his imaginative powers, she is certainly able to discern his deepest vulnerabilities. Whenever she has the chance, Lady Macbeth reminds her husband that pursuing his ambition is the manly thing to do. She claims that if it were possible, she would herself become a man so that she could carry out the acts Macbeth hesitates to commit. Although she does have a moment of comparative tenderness when she sees the sleeping Duncan and compares him to her father, she is a primary motivating force in Macbeth's relentless drive to win and retain the crown. She plays on his fears of weakness and woos him with promises of her love and affection. In addition, she convinces him that her carefully laid plans will assure success. When ghostly apparitions test Macbeth's resolve, her practical nature takes over as she urges him to dismiss these visions as mere products of the imagination. As A. C. Bradley notes in *Shakespearean Tragedy* (Meridian, 1955), Lady Macbeth "takes the superior position and assumes the direction of affairs,—appears to assume it even more than she really can, that she may spur him on. She animates him by picturing the deed as heroic, . . . while she ignores its cruelty and faithlessness."

3. *Explain the significance of the following lines as one index of the play's themes:*

> [Witches]: Fair is foul, and foul is fair.
> Hover through the fog and filthy air.

Find one or more additional passages that further establish and elaborate this theme.

The world of *Macbeth* is dark and evil. Natural order has been reversed, and nothing is as it should be. For another example of the strange setting that reflects the theme of appearance versus reality, see Act II, Scene IV, lines 6–7, where Ross says to an old man he meets:

> By th' clock 'tis day,
> And yet dark night strangles the traveling lamp:

Later, as Macbeth struggles to retain the crown and thus further pervert the established order, he observes the murky road he must traverse:

> Light thickens, and the crow
> Makes wing to th' rooky wood.
> Good things of day begin to droop and drowse,
> Whiles night's black agents to their preys do rouse.
>
> *(Act III, Scene II, Lines 50–53)*

Mark Van Doren in his essay, "Macbeth," notes that in the world of the play "nothing is certain to keep its shape. Forms shift and consistencies alter, so that what was solid may flow and what was fluid may congeal to stone" (in *Shakespeare: Modern Essays in Criticism,* Oxford University Press, 1967).

4. *Look carefully at the scenes involving the witches. What do these scenes have in common? What is their significance and their cumulative effect on characters and on the audience?*

The witches appear in Act I, Scene I; Act I, Scene III; Act III,

Scene V; and Act IV, Scene I. In the opening scene, the witches establish an unnatural atmosphere, a setting that forebodes evil, disorder, and perverted power. Their apparently positive promises in Act I, Scene III, are revealed as breeding horror in Act IV, Scene I. The characters, especially Macbeth, become increasingly obsessed with the witches as the play progresses. Macbeth allows himself to be seduced by their promises and then longs desperately to be rescued. The witches serve primarily as symbols for today's audiences, but it is worthwhile reminding students that many Elizabethans believed in the power of witches and that many "witches" were executed during that time.

5. Identify one scene in which sound is important. Explain its effect.

The thunder in the witches' scenes is extremely important. Note, for instance, how thunder punctuates the exchange between Macbeth and the witches in Act IV, Scene I.

6. Look carefully at the beginning and ending of any two acts. Explain how Shakespeare guides the audience's responses at these points.

At the beginning of Act III, Banquo's speech sums up what Macbeth has done and evaluates his actions; Lennox's moving words at the end note the suffering visited on the entire country because of Macbeth's distorted ambition. Lady Macbeth's sleepwalking scene at the beginning of Act V portends the disintegration of her household, and the doctor's words—"a great perturbation in nature" (line 8)—portend the extent of the evil that has been unleashed; Malcolm's concluding speech indicts Macbeth and Lady Macbeth, "this dead butcher and his fiendlike queen," and indicates the restoration of order to Scotland through the crowning of the new and rightful king.

7. Identify one scene in which characters' speeches shift between verse and prose. Explain the significance of this shifting.

One possibility: In Act I, Scene V, Lady Macbeth receives and reads a letter written in prose, describing the witches' prophecies. The letter's powerful message leads naturally to the poetic speech that follows: "Glamis thou art, and Cawdor, and shalt be/What thou art promised." This speech demonstrates the extent of Lady Macbeth's ambition, and its poetic rhythms emphasize its significance.

8. *Any staging of* Macbeth *requires careful attention to lighting. Single out one or two scenes in which lighting is especially important, and explain how you would stage them.*

Any of the scenes in which the witches appear would work well for this assignment.

Going Further

1. *Watch the film* Throne of Blood, *a Japanese version of* Macbeth, *and then discuss the similarities and differences between the two works.*

2. *Compare the predictions of the weird sisters in Act I with the apparitions and their prophecies in Act IV. How do the. differences in these two scenes suggest the progression of plot and the development of character?*

3. *Several characters receive news of the death of loved ones. (Macduff learns of the murder of his wife and children; Old Siward is told of his son's death; Macbeth hears that Lady Macbeth has died.) Compare the responses these characters have to their losses.*

4. *Examine the role of several minor characters. Consider, for example, Hecate. Why is she in the play? What would be lost if she were eliminated?*

5. *Reread carefully each of Macbeth's long asides and soliloquies. What changes in his character are evident in these speeches? Which of these speeches do you find most memorable? Which seems most relevant to modern times? Explain your choices.*

The Doctor in Spite of Himself

(Jean-Baptiste Poquelin) Molière (1622–1673)

Born into a respectable middle-class Parisian family in the early seventeenth century, Jean-Baptiste Poquelin was an unlikely candidate to become a celebrated playwright. Any connection with actors or the theater was considered suspect, and young Jean-Baptiste was apparently destined by his family for a career in law. Between the years of 1632 and approximately 1637 he studied at the Collège de Clermont and began legal studies. The only hint we have to suggest where his fascination with the stage originated is the story that his grandfather used to take the young scholar to watch Italian comedians and French tragedians at the Hotel de Bourgogne as a break from his studies. Whatever his reasons, we do know that Jean-Baptiste Poquelin at the age of 20 rejected the legal profession (renouncing also his right to follow his father as "upholsterer by appointment of the king") to become an actor.

His initial ventures were anything but successful, and his determination is reflected by his refusal to return to the safe (and prosperous) bosom of his family. In 1643 he was a principal founder of the Illustre Theatre, a venture that met with spectacular failure and landed Molière (the stage name he had adopted) in debtors' prison. In spite of this setback, however, Molière and the Béjart family, who had also backed the Illustre Theatre, continued to work together. Literary gossip has it that Molière was in love with Madeleine Béjart, but whether or not he lost his heart to the beautiful actress, he certainly lost it to the world of the theater. He and the Béjarts joined the Dufresne theater company in 1645 and left Paris to tour the provinces, remaining away from the city until 1658.

During those thirteen years, Molière turned to writing as a way to eke out the meager living of an actor's wages. In 1655 his troupe performed *L'Étourdi,* the first work that can definitely be attributed to Molière. In 1658 he and his troupe returned to Paris, and Molière continued to write comedies that gained great success, owing at least in part to his ability to introduce farce into plays that dealt with classic comic themes. In 1662 he wrote and produced the play that was to escalate him into controversial fame, *L'École des Femmes.* With this biting comic drama, Molière "showed that comedy, for the first time, was dangerous: it no longer involved some conventional other person but, in the very terms of the convention, the spectator himself," writes Jacques Guicharnaud in the introduction to *Molière: A Collection of Critical Essays* (Prentice-Hall, 1964).

Throughout his distinguished career, Molière continued to write sharply incisive comedies that brilliantly combined the imaginary and farcical with real truths about the lives of theatergoers. As Guicharnaud suggests, many of Molière's major plays "show that everyone's life is a romance, a farce, a disgrace."

Teaching the Play

Many students will find *The Doctor in Spite of Himself* much more accessible than Greek or Elizabethan drama. Molière's adherence to precise conventions (discussed in "Neoclassical Drama," student text pp. 55–56) does not detract from the play's appeal. In fact, students often find the number of classical elements present in seventeenth-century drama interesting.

Students can discuss the artistic and practical merits of using satire instead of persuasive essays (or any other genre) as a means of identifying problems and provoking social or political change. They can point to political cartoonists, such as Garry Trudeau, and columnists, such as Art Buchwald, as effective contemporary satirists. Most students will agree that satire, including satiric drama, can be a powerful and provocative influence in society.

Students can extend their understanding of satire by noting the techniques writers use to achieve it, such as irony, sarcasm, innuendo, and so on. Students often enjoy creating satiric skits of school and community life, ridiculing aspects of their own world. They quickly discover that preparing even very short satiric skits is extremely difficult, thus increasing their appreciation for Molière's skill.

As with Greek and Elizabethan drama, the set description and stage directions for this play are minimal. However, students will perceive that the dialogue is different—more easily understood and faster paced. Beyond this, readers are attracted by the humor in *The Doctor in Spite of Himself,* but they also understand and appreciate the underlying commentary on power structures in relationships.

The play revolves on two connected plots, the abused wife who takes revenge on her husband by claiming he is a doctor who will work miracles only when beaten, and the repressed daughter who outsmarts her dictatorial father by pretending she has lost the power of speech. Because the audience is in on the pretenses (we know that Sganarelle is no physician and that Lucinde's vocal chords function perfectly), the enjoyment comes from watching the shifts of power and the comeuppance dished out to those who most deserve it.

Summary *of* The Doctor in Spite of Himself

Act I Sganarelle and Martine argue about who got the worse deal in their marriage. Sganarelle gambles and drinks, selling off the family possessions to pay his debts. He brags about having once "served a famous doctor" (Scene I)—a boast that will return to haunt him. When he is unable to outwit Martine verbally, he starts beating her. When the beating is interrupted by M. Robert, their neighbor, both husband and wife turn on him, demanding that he keep his nose out of their business. Martine, however, harbors resentment and vows to get revenge. She soon comes upon Lucas and Valère, who are trying to find a way to cure their master's daughter, who has lost her power of speech. Martine sees her chance and tells them Sganarelle is a doctor who has miraculous powers that he will use only when beaten. Act I closes with Valère and Lucas beating a bemused Sganarelle, who admits to anything they ask—even that he is, indeed, a physician.

Act II Valère and Lucas bring Sganarelle to Géronte, their master, while Jacqueline, the wet nurse, argues that all Lucinde, the ailing daughter, needs to cure her is marriage to the right man, Léandre. Géronte counters that Lucinde should marry his choice, a man who has wealth. Sganarelle and Géronte exchange verbal thrusts as the worried father tries to assure himself of the "doctor's" credentials. Sganarelle cannot resist making lewd comments and gestures toward Jacqueline, who, from the beginning, is skeptical not only about him but also about Lucinde's illness. When Sganarelle is brought to the patient, he responds with hilarious mumbo jumbo combining elementary Latin phrases with pseudomedical jargon designed to impress Géronte. Lucinde responds to his comments and questions only by pointing and grunting, yet everyone is impressed by the slick posturing and pronouncement of Sganarelle. Géronte pays the "doctor" handsomely, and as he walks away counting his booty, he is waylaid by Léandre, who begs his help in carrying out a scheme to marry Lucinde. At first Sganarelle refuses, but he quickly changes his mind when Léandre offers a generous bribe.

Act III In return for Léandre's revealing that Lucinde's illness is feigned, Sganarelle admits that he is not really a doctor. While he consults with some peasants come to seek his advice, he sends Léandre, disguised as an apothecary, to Géronte's house. Sganarelle then proceeds to Géronte's, where he flirts outrageously with Jacqueline, encouraging her to betray her jealous husband by making him wear the cuckold's horns (". . . he would also deserve to have you plant a certain decoration on his head, to punish him for his suspicions," Scene III). Lucas interrupts his wife and the "doctor" just as Géronte comes looking for Sganarelle. Lucinde takes a walk with the apothecary (her would-be lover, Léandre) and suddenly begins a vehement argument against marrying her father's chosen suitor. Géronte is amazed at his daughter's sudden recovery but remains adamant that she marry the wealthy Horace. Disturbed at his daughter's vituperative comments, Géronte begs Sganarelle to "cut this illness of the mind" (Scene VI). The "doctor" prescribes "a dose of purgative flight" combined with "two drams of matrimonium . . ." and thus sends the young lovers off to be secretly married. When Géronte discovers the ruse, he vows to have Sganarelle hanged. Martine arrives and shows little sympathy for her husband's plight. All is resolved when Léandre returns with Lucinde, vowing he will marry her honorably and announcing that he has inherited the property of his uncle, who has just died. Géronte is now perfectly satisfied with the match, and Martine claims credit for having made Sganarelle a doctor, a profession he intends to continue practicing.

Discussion and Writing Topics

1. *Identify the sources of the play's humor. What do you find amusing, and why? Characterize the style of the play's humor.*

The humor in *The Doctor in Spite of Himself* relies heavily on word play and purposely misunderstood meanings. For example, in the opening scene, when Martine accuses Sganarelle of eating up everything she owns, he replies, "That's a lie: I drink part of it." And of course the wonderful scene when Sganarelle bamboozles everyone with his fancy Latinesque rap, as well as the interlude when the peasant Thibaut offers a twisted disgression on his wife's illness, show the power of Molière's verbal wit. Humor also comes from the action of the play—the beatings, which are varieties of Punch-and-Judy exchanges, and Sganarelle's falling over in his chair suggest the slapstick of many modern film comedies (students will easily provide examples; John Candy and Dan Ackroyd are masters of this genre). Another source of humor, more subtle and enjoyed as one contemplates the play after having read or seen it, is its irony. The reversals come in almost dizzying succession. The beater becomes the beaten; the quack becomes the true curer; the nurse who proclaims the sanctity of marriage and of marrying for love is only too willing to betray her husband. And of course no one can overlook the cynicism of the "happily ever after" marriage. Géronte is satisfied with Léandre only after the latter becomes heir to a fortune, and even Léandre apparently becomes an honest suitor only when he knows that, because of the rich uncle's timely death, he will be accepted by his greedy future father-in-law.

2. *Are there any parts of the play that seem intended to be humorous but that you do not find funny? Explain your answer.*

Many students will question the opening scenes, which not only make a joke of wife-beating but also suggest that the wife really likes to be beaten (or at least that she does not want anyone to interfere with her husband's "rights"). At a time when so much exposure is being given to battered wives (and when many students may have witnessed domestic violence themselves), it is hard to laugh as unreservedly at the exchanges between Martine and Sganarelle as Molière's original audience no doubt did. Martine's later actions, of course, show that she really does not like being beaten and that she harbors well-founded resentments. Her complaints against her husband will seem far more serious to students of the 1990s than will his implication that he was disappointed in his wedding night (possibly she was not a virgin).

Another scene that strikes many as cruel—and a scene that is frequently cut when the play is performed today—is the interlude with the peasants (Act III, Scene II). Sganarelle is not hurting anyone when he pretends to cure Lucinde (who is not really ill), but he is certainly guilty of practicing fraud when he sends the "miraculous" cheese home with Thibaut and Perrin to cure their seriously ill wife and mother. And the callous comment he calls after them as a farewell, "If she dies, don't fail to give her the best burial you can," will strike many as gratuitously cruel rather than funny.

3. *What is Molière's attitude toward doctors? What ideas about medicine and doctors emerge in the play? Are any of these current or relevant today? Explain your answer.*

The characters in the play, whether they are peasants or landed gentry, accept Sganarelle's word as absolute truth because they assume he is a doctor. They believe his persiflage. When he speaks a mumbo jumbo of butchered Latin phrases, they admire him as wise:

> Jacqueline: Oh! That man of ourn! Ain't that well said?
> *(Act II, Scene IV)*

And even when he presents information contrary to what they know to be the truth, they are easily convinced that the "doctor" is right. For instance, when Sganarelle mistakes the location of the liver and the heart, Géronte questions him, but immediately retreats with humble apologies. Referring to the position of the vital organs, Sganarelle says, "Yes, it used to be that way; but we have changed all that, and now we practice medicine in a completely new way." Much abashed, Géronte replies, "That's something I didn't know, and I beg your pardon for my ignorance" (Act II, Scene IV).

If we can assume that Molière shares the view of doctors offered by Sganarelle's impersonation and the other characters' ready acceptance of that posture, then the playwright clearly saw physicians as arrogant, stuffy, phony purveyors of false hope and ludicrous remedies. Molière was himself plagued by illness, and perhaps his poor health, necessitating visits to doctors, contributed to his attitude. In any case, we know that he satirized the medical profession in several of his plays. Here is what J. D. Jubert observes about another of Molière's doctors: In his "specialized universe, only the hierarchy of medicine and disease really matters. Physicians have discretionary powers, and the patient must obey them

MOLIÈRE

without a murmur" ("The Doctor's Curse" in *Molière: A Collection of Critical Essays*).

Students' opinions will vary, of course, as to whether any of the attitudes toward doctors and medicine are relevant today, but most will agree that far too many people still accept the word of their physician as law and are afraid to question or to seek a second opinion. On the other hand, modern malpractice suits and the like show that at least some patients are not willing to sit back and allow their doctors to do anything they want.

4. *What role does Monsieur Robert play? Could he be eliminated? Explain your answer.*

M. Robert is much more important to the play than he may seem at first. He is not just a part of the plot mechanism, but rather he provides the audience an essential view of Martine's character. Without M. Robert's intervention, Martine would probably be cast in an entirely sympathetic role. She is, after all, the victim of her husband's neglect and bad habits. Yet when she turns on M. Robert and treats him exactly as she has been treated (she slaps him soundly for "interfering"), we see that she too has an irrational and violent way of viewing the world. The interaction between M. Robert and Martine prepares us for the central complication of the play, Martine's attempt to get revenge on her husband. M. Robert, then, is not merely written into the play for comic diversion (as, for example, are Thibaut and Perrin) but rather to serve an essential role.

5. *Explain how Molière arranges the incidents of the play to build toward the climax.*

The play is built on a series of revenge schemes, pretenses, and officious actions. See pages 52–53 of this guide for a detailed summary of the action leading to the climax, in Act III, Scene VI, when Sganarelle, now accepting the role of doctor forced upon him, sends the would-be lovers off for "two drams of matrimonium." The play's comic resolution comes not from resisting illusion but from accepting the fantasy (that Sganarelle is a doctor) and using it to advantage.

6. *Select one scene, and explain how you would stage it. Consider especially the physical movements of the actors.*

Students may enjoy staging Act I, Scene V, where Valère and Lucas beat Sganarelle into admitting that he is a physician. Another likely possibility is Act III, Scene III, when Sganarelle flirts with Jacqueline while her jealous husband lurks in the background.

Going Further

1. *Research the occupation of wet-nurse. Why is it significant that Jacqueline is a wet-nurse? How does Molière use her profession to create some of the play's humor?*

2. *This play has been translated into what is supposedly modern English, yet some of the phrases are clearly dated. Find some of these speeches (for instance, at the beginning of Act I, Scene IV, when Lucas says,"Doggone it! We sure both tooken on one heck of a job"). Then try your hand at revising them into current vernacular (remembering to maintain the original tone and meaning).*

3. *Both Shakespeare in* Macbeth *and Molière in* The Doctor in Spite of Himself *work with the theme of appearance versus reality. Things are not as they seem to be, and natural order is reversed. Compare Shakespeare's treatment of this theme with Molière's.*

4. *What are the two plots of the play? Are they equally important, or is one a subplot? Discuss their relationship and what they suggest about the theme of the play.*

5. *Do some research on medical practices in the seventeenth century. For example, consider the theory of bodily humors. How does Molière use these medical practices to develop character and to provide plot developments? What has happened to such theories and practices today? Have they been entirely discarded, or do some of them remain either in their original or in a modified form?*

An Enemy of the People

Henrik Ibsen (1828–1906)

During Henrik Ibsen's earliest years, his father was a prosperous merchant. In 1836, however, he filed for bankruptcy, and the family was forced to move to a small farm outside of the town of Skien in Norway. Because of the sudden change in fortune, Ibsen attended a public school, where he felt he received an inferior education. He seems never to have recovered from the shame this economic reversal brought him, and as soon as he was old enough, he struck out on his own, becoming a druggist's apprentice and, according to his close friends, returning to visit his family only once.

During his years as an apprentice, he led an unconventional life and was a founding member of a radical club that worked for issues of personal and national freedom. In addition to his political activism, he also showed himself to be a social rebel in the traditional way of young men—he drank and gambled heavily and at age 18 admitted to being an unwed father. In spite of his resistance to conventional behavior, he longed to better himself intellectually and studied for entrance exams at the University of Christiania. He never completed the exams, but in 1850 he wrote his first play, *Catiline*. From 1851 to 1857 he worked as a stage manager (a job that included directing). In 1857 he moved to what is now Oslo, where he became director of the Norwegian Theater. In that capacity he wrote plays, as well as directing them. In 1858 he married Susannah Thoresen. Following the bankruptcy of the Norwegian Theater and political disappointments (specifically the refusal of the Norwegian government to fight with the Danes against Prussia in 1863), he and his family moved abroad, living primarily in Italy, until 1891.

While abroad, he wrote prolifically, creating such works as *Peer Gynt* (1867), *A Doll's House* (1879), *Ghosts* (1881), and *An Enemy of the People* (1882).

In the years following *Enemy,* Ibsen wrote plays at the average rate of one every other year, ending with *When We Dead Awaken* in 1899. He had returned to Norway in 1891, where he lived quietly until he suffered a stroke in 1900, which left him an invalid until his death in 1906.

Ibsen was a major pioneer in the modern realistic theater and, indeed, in theater history. Another master of modern drama, Luigi Pirandello, proclaimed, "After Shakespeare, I put Ibsen first."

Teaching the Play

Ibsen's plays were frequently controversial. *A Doll's House* offended traditional thinkers by showing as its heroine a wife who leaves her husband and children. The outcry against this play was so great that Ibsen was coerced into writing an alternative ending in which Nora, the wife, returns to her family. *Ghosts,* which addresses the problem of venereal disease, managed to alienate most of those who had stayed loyal through the furor over *A Doll's House.* Perhaps Ibsen's experiences with these two plays and the public's response contributed to his desire to write *An Enemy of the People,* which shows an idealistic reformer who is vilified by the very individuals he seeks to help.

In addition to Ibsen's own experiences, we know that *Enemy* is based on other episodes from real life. In *Ibsen and Strindberg* (Cassell, 1962), F. L. Lucas tells us:

> Ibsen had heard of a certain Dr. Meissner at Teplitz whose house was stoned in the thirties, because he reported an outbreak of cholera, and so ruined the spa's season. Also a certain Thaulow (1815–81), an apothecary in Christiania, who had a long feud with the Christiania Steam Kitchen . . . had been howled down at a public meeting . . . and died a fortnight later.

Students may be interested to know that when *Enemy* was performed at the Moscow Art Theater in 1905 on the day a group of revolutionaries were massacred, members of the audience cheered furiously and jumped onstage to shake the hand and slap the back of the actor playing the Doctor's role. Many other idealists throughout the decades to follow have identified equally strongly with Ibsen's gentle idealist.

Summary of An Enemy of the People

Act I The exposition of the play takes place during an evening gathering at the home of Thomas and Katherine Stockmann. We learn that the town has built new baths (a spa), which Dr. Stockmann has helped to design. His older brother, Peter Stockmann, who holds the office of mayor as well as several political titles, shows his politic and conservative nature by praising Hovstad, the editor of the local newspaper, while taking most of the credit for the baths himself. Dr. Stockmann suggests that there might be some problems with the baths; his brother warns him that whatever ideas the Doctor has, he must go through the proper channels with them. The Mayor leaves and Hovstad and his assistant, Billing, show themselves to be fainthearted opportunists when they express patriotic views to Captain Horster, whom they take for a conservative, but volunteer liberal views to the freethinking Stockmann daughter, Petra. Dr. Stockmann reads a letter Petra has brought him and announces that the baths are polluted by drainage from nearby tanneries (the largest of which, we later learn, is owned by Morten Kiil, Mrs. Stockmann's foster father). The Doctor believes he has made a discovery that will bring him adulation and praise because it will save a great many lives, and the first act ends with him and Katherine dancing around the room.

Act II Morten Kiil arrives at the Stockmann's home the next morning, delighted over Dr. Stockmann's insistence that the baths are polluted since he holds a grudge against the main town politicians and the baths committee. Hovstad arrives and expresses moral indignation, comparing the poison in the baths' water to the corruption that pervades the town government. He portrays himself as the appropriate person to liberate (through his journalism) the common people. Aslaksen, the printer, joins them to offer his moderate support. He warns against alienating the authorities and tries to convince the Doctor that such action will not be necessary because the "solid majority" of middle-class people will support the need to clean up the baths. Dr. Stockmann is elated to contemplate such backing, but Katherine Stockmann innocently questions whether the support of the solid majority is a good thing. Her unwittingly shrewd insight serves as a foreshadowing for the play's resolution. Next the Mayor arrives, very angry about the Doctor's report. He insists that he and other town officials be left to handle the problem. Because the Doctor refuses to retract his accusations, his brother pronounces him an enemy of society.

Act III In this act, which takes place at the newspaper office, the central characters show their true colors. Hovstad and Billing, who pretend to liberal views, demonstrate that they are interested mainly in bettering their own personal, professional, or political situations. Billing, for instance, is hoping for a position in the local government. Hovstad tells Petra that he has supported her father primarily because he is interested in her. And Aslaksen glosses his theme of moderation by explaining that he is liberal on national issues but rather conservative on local issues because no one cares what one thinks about national politics but opposition to local officials could cause recriminations. Petra, on the other hand, shows herself to be her father's daughter by refusing to translate for Hovstad's newspaper a story she considers to be unrealistic. When the Mayor arrives and informs Aslaksen and Hovstad that any improvements to the baths will have to be paid for by the taxpayers, they turn against the Doctor and refuse to print his report. The act ends with the Mayor raging against his brother and with everyone turning against Thomas Stockmann except his wife and daughter.

Act IV The townspeople gather at Captain Horster's house. Only he has been willing to offer space for the Doctor to present his report. Even before the Doctor can begin speaking, however, Aslaksen is elected chairman of the meeting, and the Mayor tries to block his brother's speech. When the Doctor claims his subject is not the polluted baths, he is allowed to address the group, and he delivers a ringing denouncement of the social framework of the entire community. He is particularly hard, not on the town officials (whom he regards as rather dull-witted), but on the solid majority, who, he claims, accept only traditional (and often outmoded) ideas as true. The Doctor develops an elaborate analogy between humans and animals, claiming that well-bred dogs, for instance, are far superior to common mutts. Therefore, he claims, the intellectuals among humans (a minority) are also superior because they do not simply follow the tried-and-true ways but look for new ways to solve both old and new problems. Dr. Stockmann declares that he would rather see the town destroyed than to see it prosper on a base of corruption and lies (referring both to the baths and to the corrupt government). When Aslaksen calls for a vote, the Doctor is officially declared "an enemy of the people," and he is jeered and insulted as the meeting comes to a close.

Act V In the poignant and memorable opening scene, Dr. Stockmann walks around his wrecked study. His wife brings notice that they are being evicted because the landlord "doesn't dare not to" send them on their way. This message establishes a motif for the scene: Petra is dismissed from her teaching position because the school directors "don't dare not to"; Captain Horster (who remains the Doctor's friend) is fired from his position as ship's captain because the ship's owner "doesn't dare not to." The final note of this motif is sounded by the Mayor, who brings a letter of dismissal to his brother because he "doesn't dare not to." The moral weakness displayed by these conformists to the opinion of the solid majority underlines the Doctor's earlier wry comment (as he regards his torn clothing and ruined home) that one should never wear his best trousers when going out to fight for truth and freedom.

Morten Kiil now comes and threatens the Doctor by telling him that he has spent all the money that was destined for Katherine and their sons on stock in the baths. If Thomas does not renounce his position, not only will he be ruined, but he will also ruin all future hope for his wife and sons.

Hovstad and Aslaksen try to reap profit from the Doctor's misfortunes and once again demonstrate their lack of moral fiber. In a marvelously comic scene, Thomas drives them out of his house with blows from his umbrella.

When the Stockmann sons are sent home from school, the Doctor suddenly knows what he will do with his life. He will open a school to teach them, and other poor boys, to become "free-spirited and accomplished men." The play ends with the Stockmann family united and Thomas declaring that "the strongest man in the world is the one who stands most alone."

Discussion and Writing Topics

1. *What does it mean to be an "enemy of the people"? In what sense can either the Doctor or the Mayor (or both) be considered such an enemy? Explain your answer.*

Responses will, of course, vary widely. Because Dr. Stockmann is portrayed so sympathetically, students will probably see his being designated an "enemy" as richly ironic. Nevertheless, some dissenters may note that a person who follows the path of uncompromising truth can often bring pain and suffering to those who least deserve it. Certainly we do not spend a lot of time thinking about the impact that closing the baths will have on the economy of the community, and that lack is due at least in part to the emphasis Ibsen places on the human goodness of the Doctor. We never wonder why he doesn't spend some of his emotional agonizing on thoughts of those who are innocent of wrongdoing yet would be hurt if he accomplished his goals. Students may be interested to know that Ibsen himself was intrigued by the implications of the absolutist view and that in his next play, *The Wild Duck,* he explored the evil effects of an insistence on strict adherence to a moral code. (His earlier play, *Brand,* also investigates this theme.)

It is much easier, of course, to see the Doctor's brother, Peter Stockmann, as an enemy of the people. He represents the shrewd politician who watches out for the townspeople only so that he can continue to hold a position of authority. Though it seems to the solid majority that the Mayor is protecting their best interests, he is, of course, concerned mainly with himself. Peter Stockmann guards the economic welfare of the town, and most of the people are satisfied with such a surface approach. They do not want to question their values or to sacrifice comfort in order to behave morally. The reader of this play probably holds an opinion different from the townspeople, seeing the Mayor as an "enemy of the people" in the most profound sense. He refuses to lead them to more decent lives, preferring instead to promote the comfortable status quo. Students will have no trouble making comparisons with modern-day politicians and the choices they make.

2. *Peter and Thomas Stockmann are clearly opposite characters with radically different temperaments and personalities. Describe their differences, and identify what each character represents.*

Dr. Stockmann is a reformer and a liberal. He constantly fights for truth and social justice, yet he has none of the grimmer characteristics that often typify morally righteous people. For example, he clearly enjoys the small pleasures he is now able to afford because of his financially comfortable position. He is a genial host and an attentive, caring father and husband. Because the Doctor does not try to temper or hide his idealism, he constantly finds himself in trouble with authority figures. He often sees—and tells—the truth when others do not. Yet he does not assume the stature of a wise, heroic martyr filled with knowledge and vision because he also shows a distinctly naive side of himself. For instance, for most of the play he allows himself to be duped by Hovstad and Billing in their schemes to gain power and recognition for themselves. No matter what happens, Thomas Stockmann always takes an optimistic, almost childlike view of the situation, and even at the end of the play when he faces financial ruin, he is able to maintain his integrity and to declare his intention to start over with a new career.

Peter Stockmann, the Mayor, is a nearly exact opposite of his brother. He is a conservative politician whose main interest lies in conserving wealth and power for himself and for those who support him. In the opening scene, he shows that he disapproves of his brother's open, generous life-style by suggesting that hot beef is excessive as an evening meal. Whereas Thomas never thinks about his own reputation or his own welfare when he is faced with a moral question, Peter thinks primarily about himself. The Mayor is quite willing to sacrifice the health of those who will use the baths to spare himself the embarrassment and expense of having renovations made to prevent the pollution. Peter Stockmann is shrewd and worldly; he understands how to manipulate people to get what he wants. Unlike his optimistic brother, he tends to put the worst possible face on a situation. For example, he imagines the ruin of the entire town if the news of the polluted baths gets out. The Mayor has no interest in social concerns or in any larger good. He cares only for himself.

The two brothers clearly represent the opposite poles of public men. The Mayor actually holds office, yet is selfish and derelict in his duties. The Doctor, on the other hand, acts for the public welfare as an unelected individual who simply cares a great deal about following the path of moral action. Although it is an oversimplification, we might designate Thomas as an idealist and Peter as an opportunist.

3. *What function in the dramatic or symbolic action of the play do the following characters serve: Hovstad, Aslaksen, Petra, Captain Horster?*

In the first act we see Hovstad and his associate, Billing, accepting the Doctor's hospitality and apparently sharing his liberal views. They show their true colors, of course, when they begin a conversation with Captain Horster and fit their comments to what they believe the Captain's patriotic beliefs to be. We also see in Act III that Hovstad has few scruples or ideals concerning his editing. He admonishes Petra when she refuses to translate an overly sentimental piece of writing, telling her that he prints what his readers want to hear. Later in the play he betrays his friendship with the Doctor, accusing Thomas of misrepresentation. The accusation, of course, merely covers his desire to switch alliances to what he now believes will be the winning side. (Students may be interested to know that Ibsen had become disillusioned with lip-service liberals who wavered back and forth on moral issues when many so-called liberals failed to support him in his fight against the storm of criticism leveled against his play *Ghosts,* which dealt frankly with venereal disease.) Aslaksen is primarily a comic character, but through him Ibsen satirizes middle-class conformity. The printer goes to great lengths to explain that he supports idealistic views concerning national affairs, but in local affairs, where he might be criticized or shunned, he supports "moderation." This word becomes his trademark. No matter how serious or how corrupt the circumstance, he urges "moderation." When the Doctor beats Aslaksen out of his house as the latter still proclaims "moderation," we see Ibsen soundly banishing the voice of shallow mediocrity.

Petra is an intriguing character who shows us a great deal about herself as well as about her mother and father and the family in which she was raised. First, she has been educated and now holds a teaching position. We can see that in a society where women were still distinctly second-class citizens, Katherine and Thomas Stockmann were determined to give their daughter every possible opportunity to develop her talents. Few women worked outside the home at that time and certainly very few women who were part of an upper middle-class family. Petra clearly enjoys her work, and, in addition, she shows herself to have the same integrity as her father when she refuses the translating job because she considers the story inferior. Unlike her father, however, she sees quite soon the shoddy character of those who try to deceive her. When Hovstad tries to sweet-talk her into continuing the translation, she is not flattered and encouraged. Instead, she declares her disillusion and walks out. Like her mother, Petra is loyal and loving toward Thomas. She sees his idiosyncrasies, but stands by him completely, even when she loses her teaching position because of his moral stand. Petra seems almost to enjoy the challenge her family faces.

Captain Horster is interesting because he seems relatively apolitical. Nevertheless, he enjoys the camaraderie and friendship of the highly political Doctor. It is interesting to note that at the end of Act IV Thomas imagines going to America with Captain Horster. Shortly thereafter, we learn that Captain Horster has been dismissed from his position because of his association with the Doctor. The Captain, who could not be considered a political liberal and who certainly does not claim to be one, remains loyal when those who supposedly shared Thomas's philosophy have deserted him.

4. *Identify one or more humorous aspects of the play. In what sense, if any, can* Enemy *be considered a "comedy"?*

Though there are certainly tragic elements in *Enemy,* it can be viewed as having a comic vision. Many of the scenes and characteristics are subtly funny (for instance, the pompous Peter grumping in Act I about hot meat and the amount of money his brother spends while nonetheless enjoying his hospitality). Other scenes are filled with black humor (for instance, the scene in Act V where the Doctor sadly surveys his wrecked study and comments bemusedly that "[o]ne should never wear his best trousers when he goes out fighting for truth and freedom"). Of course, the play also contains wonderful slapstick scenes. One of the best occurs when Dr. Stockmann takes his umbrella in hand and beats the smarmy Aslaksen from his house.

Finally, there is the ending of the play. It is the conclusion that really determines whether a drama is comic or tragic. The hero certainly has suffered setbacks and enormous disappointments, but we have no sense that he is defeated. Instead, he appears as a noble figure who will carry on and continue to fight. The forces of good have not been banished. And although evil has not been conquered, either, we know that it will not be left to flourish in peace. In the traditional Shakespearean comedy and in Restoration comedies, the drama traditionally ended with a reconciling marriage. Thomas is, of course, already happily married, yet the final scene with his family gathered around him in support certainly echoes the loving unity of the conventional comic ending.

Ibsen himself, by the way, was not sure how to define *Enemy*. In a letter written in June 1882, he said that he did not know whether to call this work a tragedy or a comedy since "it partakes of the nature of either, or lies half way between" (quoted by Janko Lavrin in *Ibsen: An Approach,* Russell and Russell, 1969).

5. How do the baths serve as an underlying metaphor for the play?

The baths issue from water that runs under the town and that has now become polluted from the industrial waste produced by Morten Kiil's tannery, among others. Greed, then, initiates the pollution. The town officials, typified by Peter Stockmann, refuse to do anything about the problem because it would be too costly both economically and professionally. Greed, again. Finally, the solid majority throws its support to the forces represented by Kiil and the Mayor because its members do not want to face paying the price their Mayor has promised them will be extracted. Greed and self-interest motivate the responses of everyone in the town with the exception of Katherine and Thomas Stockmann and their family (and Captain Horster). The polluted baths come to symbolize the moral foundation of the town itself, which is also corrupt. This analogy, of course, is suggested by Hovstad in Act II and again by the Doctor's climactic speech in Act IV.

6. Examine the plot of the play. How does Ibsen control our responses and arouse our curiosity? Indicate places where the tempo of the play increases, and explain the effect of those changes.

The action quickens at the end of Act II when the Mayor insists that the Doctor retract his views on the baths. Peter Stockmann's threat to dismiss his brother heightens the reader/viewer's curiosity about the outcome of the Doctor's campaign. Again in Act IV, the public meeting gains in intensity, climaxing with the Doctor's being declared "an enemy of the people." Once again we wonder whether he will continue to hold tight to his views in the face of increasing opposition. Finally, in Act V, one indignity and loss after another are piled on the Doctor and his family. We read/view eagerly, anxious to understand the fate of this idealistic man.

7. *Act IV shows us a town meeting. What image of the towns-people are we given there? How does Ibsen convey that image?*

The crowd is rude and boorish, interrupting the Doctor's speech with shouted insults. Dr. Stockmann compares the townspeople to ill-bred animals and places the responsibility for their willingness to ignore the pollution squarely on their shoulders (and not on the corrupt officials like the Mayor). The townspeople show themselves to be interested mainly in money and in maintaining the status quo rather than in understanding what is right.

8. *Identify two visual details or objects, and explain their dramatic or symbolic significance.*

In Act III, Dr. Stockmann happily picks up his brother's staff and hat and walks grandly around the room as though he enjoyed the splendor of public office. The others are embarrassed for him, but we know that he in fact has concern for the public's welfare in a way his brother does not. In Act V, the Doctor picks a stone up from his study floor, recognizing its significance as a violent symbol of the townspeople's hatred. He understands that he can no longer continue living with the illusion that people want to know the truth; the stone has broken his protective shield of innocence as well as the window of his study.

9. *Single out an important scene, and explain how you would stage it. Pay special attention to props and the facial expressions of the actors.*

The scene in Act III where Petra confronts Hovstad with the manuscript of the English story is lively, as is the town meeting in Act IV; and students should really enjoy staging the Doctor's final confrontation with Hovstad and Aslaksen in Act V, as he beats them both out of his house with his umbrella.

Going Further

   1. *The Doctor must make many difficult choices among loyalties to his fellow townspeople, to his family, and to his professional obligation as a doctor. Do you think he makes the right choices? Are there any other choices he could have made so that the problem of the baths might have been solved differently? Explain your answer.*

   2. *Katherine Stockmann changes her attitude toward her husband's actions. In Act III she cautions him not to do anything that might hurt the family, yet in Act IV she stands behind him. Do you find this change believable? Why do you think Katherine changes in this way?*

   3. *Analyze the character of Morten Kiil. Why is he in the play? What would be lost if he were not related to Katherine Stockmann? Why is he portrayed as her foster father rather than as a blood relative?*

   4. *During his lecture in Act IV, Dr. Stockmann argues that just as well-bred animals are more productive and intelligent than common breeds, so too is the intellectual minority more capable of making wise decisions than is the solid majority. Do you agree? Explain your answer with examples from history or from contemporary times.*

   5. *Antigonê and Dr. Stockmann are both denounced as enemies of the people. Compare these two characters, noting the conflicts they face, the individuals they oppose, the choices they make, and their circumstances at the end of the drama.*

The Stronger

August Strindberg (1849–1912)

August Strindberg's life was as intense and anguished as his drama. He has attracted droves of biographers over the years and during his own lifetime wrote nine autobiographical books. Born the fourth in a family of twelve children in Stockholm, Sweden, Strindberg was 4 years old when his father declared bankruptcy and 13 when his mother died. The playwright sums up his childhood by claiming that he "was afraid of his brothers' fists, of the girls' hairpulling, of his grandmother's snubs, of his mother's birch, of his father's cane" (quoted by F. L. Lucas in *Ibsen and Strindberg,* Cassell, 1962). How much this tortured early life affected him can only be speculated, but certainly he grew to be a strange and haunted (although certainly gifted) adult.

He adopted (and discarded) a series of religious beliefs and was by turn Buddhist, Roman Catholic, and atheist (among others). Strindberg's relationships with women were distinctly strange. We can perhaps best understand the perplexity and frustration of his three wives and many lovers by considering this anecdote from Lucas' book concerning his second wife. Strindberg had left Frida behind while he took a vacation with friends. After a few days he complained that he had had no mail from his wife. When six days passed with no letter, he declared the circumstance grounds for divorce. His friends, trying to comfort him, suggested that Frida might not know their exact location and asked if he were sure he had given her the address. His response suggests both his eccentricity and his need to dominate: "I did *not!* Am I bound to render account to my wife of where I go to stay!"

In addition to his domineering qualities, he also entertained mad fantasies. For example, when his first child, a daughter, died shortly after birth, he tortured himself by insisting that his wish for her death had killed her. Even before this mental breakdown in the 1890s, he had been deeply superstitious, imagining that advertising signs or initials written on walls contained hidden messages predicting and dictating his future actions.

If any theme runs through these bizarre adventures, it is Strindberg's problems with women. Whether he was fearing his mother's birch, railing against her death (or against the stepmother who replaced her in one year's time), or abusing one of his wives or mistresses, he showed his misogyny. This quality runs through many of his plays. The mean-spirited and domineering Mrs. X in *The Stronger* serves as a prototype for the way Strindberg viewed what the nineteenth century called "the new woman."

Teaching the Play

The Stronger demonstrates Strindberg's experimental approach to drama. The two characters are named symbolically rather than realistically, the set is starkly simple, and the action comprises entirely the monologue of one character who "talks at" the other for the duration of the drama.

Summary of The Stronger

Beginning with Mrs. X's earliest speeches, she seems the stereotyped bitch who pushes every emotional button she can find in her verbal envelopment of Miss Y. Mrs. X taunts her companion by reminding her that she has been dismissed from her acting position and that she has missed the chance to be married and have children (unlike Mrs. X, who brags about the gifts she has purchased for her offspring). The violence of this outwardly civilized meeting is underscored by the toy gun Mrs. X pulls from her bag. Her comments indicate that Miss Y has feared a real gun, a foreshadowing that alerts us to watch for motivations for Miss Y's defensive reaction.

Mrs. X continues with a bitterly humorous description of her husband, suggesting that he is a pompous fool who rants at the servants yet who behaves himself despite the great temptations offered him by luscious young actresses hungry for the theater roles they believe he controls. This speech leads Mrs. X to speculate that even Miss Y might have tried her wiles on Mr. X (Bob).

In the next speech Mrs. X thinks retrospectively about her relationship with Miss Y, admitting that the first time she saw Miss Y she was frightened of her. Mrs. X does not specify why she felt that way, but she goes on to summarize the relationship among herself, her husband, and Miss Y. As she is speaking, she sees that once Miss Y announced her engagement (which she later broke off), Mr. X and Miss Y developed "a violent friendship." This observation leads Mrs. X to surmise an affair between Miss Y and her husband.

Mrs. X then goes on to a horrific tirade in which she accuses Miss Y of invading and controlling her entire life. Mrs. X must embroider tulips because Miss Y likes them, drink chocolate because Miss Y prefers that beverage, and even name her son Eskil after Miss Y's father. After unloading her vitriolic rant, Mrs. X reconsiders and changes her tactics, returning nearly to her opening tone. She claims to pity Miss Y and once again reminds her of all she does not have: career, husband, child. She even expresses disdain for Miss Y's silence (which has eloquently dominated the entire diatribe). Mrs. X, who throughout the play has condescendingly dismissed her husband, now professes to love him and declares her intention to return home to his arms.

Discussion and Writing Topics

1. Besides the two characters onstage, a third person figures prominently in this play. What kind of person is Mr. X (Bob), whom we never see but about whom we hear so much? What kind of relationship does he have with each of the women?

It is difficult to assess Mr. X accurately since we know only what Mrs. X tells us about him. We must base our judgment on an unreliable narrator and highly contradictory pictures. For instance, in the early part of her monologue, Mrs. X pictures Mr. X as a comic bombast who imagines he controls his household by insulting the servants behind their backs. He seems a blustery coward. In the next breath, Mrs. X assures Miss Y (and herself) that her husband has never cheated on her. Since we later come to suspect strongly that he has, in fact, had an affair with Miss Y, we can hardly find this characterization entirely credible. Still, we are left to wonder. Was the affair with Miss Y an unusual event, a truly loving relationship that Mr. X allowed himself to feel only when she was apparently "safely" engaged? Or are we to believe that it is just as likely that he had an affair with the would-be actress Frédérique? Miss Y's lack of success in the theater and Mrs. X's implication that the "violent friendship" between her and Mr. X is over suggest that he may be simply a cold-hearted user who welcomes unencumbered relationships and that he may promise roles he has no power to deliver to lure unwitting young actresses. In her final speech of the play, Mrs. X proclaims her husband to be a wonderful lover (taught "how to love" by Miss Y) to whom she now wishes to return. This saccharine portrait is extremely hard to believe and is almost certainly a bitter rationalization aimed partly at convincing herself that she has won out over Miss Y and partly at providing a final, killing shot to any shred of self-esteem Miss Y may have left.

2. *To what extent does Mrs. X rationalize her husband's behavior and deceive herself? To what extent does she face the apparent truth about him, about Miss Y, and about herself?*

Although we are never entirely sure what the "truth" is, Mrs. X's mode seems to be primarily rationalization. Certainly the early speech about Mr. X rationalizes his relationships with women. Note the speech that begins, "And when he gets angry . . ." and the long speech after that beginning, "And when he comes home, he goes hunting for his slippers. . . ." Here she first makes Mr. X (Bob) sound foolish, and then she goes on to describe how he admits honestly to the temptations he faces from young actresses. If Bob does make such admissions, the chances are that he does so to avert his wife's growing suspicions. Mrs. X, however, rationalizes his ploy as simple frankness, with the explanations offered to prevent the sting of any gossip Mrs. X may hear. At the end of the play, her rationalization is quite different. She then acknowledges that Bob has cheated on her, but she puts the best possible face on the affair, taunting Miss Y with the idea that the illicit relationship is over and that she, Mrs. X, will benefit after all because Miss Y has taught her husband "how to love."

Only in the speech beginning "Our relationship was such a strange one . . ." and in the first part of the speech beginning "Don't speak! You needn't say a word!" does Mrs. X appear to understand and acknowledge the truth both to herself and to Miss Y. She admits that when she first met Miss Y she "was so frightened that I didn't dare let you out of my sight." Certainly that fear indicates a foreshadowing of the danger Miss Y proved to be. In addition to her relationship with Mr. X, we learn that Miss Y also seduced (in the emotional sense) Mrs. X. The betrayal of the affair, then, was a double treachery that Mrs. X finds painfully difficult to admit.

3. *Who is the "stronger" of the title — Miss Y or Mrs. X? Why?*

Most students will see Miss Y as the stronger. Her silence is eloquent and powerful, and one imagines an extremely talented actress with a wide range of pantomime skills playing the role. A shrug, a lifted eyebrow, or a series of increasingly loud laughs allow Miss Y to express her responses more intensely than she might have with words. Mrs. X, or course, claims to have won the battle because Miss Y is no longer involved with Mr. X. What Mrs. X does not acknowledge is her own painful recognition of weakness that results from her having been disillusioned both by her husband and by Miss Y, whom she has both feared and admired. By remaining silent, Miss Y neither agrees to nor denies Mrs. X's charges. Miss Y seems to put herself above the emotional ranting of Mrs. X and to suggest that she has made peace with herself.

On the other hand, some students may see Miss Y's silence as a kind of defeat. After all, she no longer has a relationship with Mr. X, and there is evidence to suggest that she may have been just one of many to him. If Mr. X is viewed as a "prize," Miss Y certainly does not win the confrontation. She is left with her career ruined and her engagement broken, alone on Christmas Eve. Her silence may indicate an emotional death that permits only outward, ironic gestures and has left no life within. In this alternative (and somewhat less plausible) reading, Mrs. X would be seen as the stronger because she has managed to endure in the relationship she desires. Unlike Miss Y, she has a career, a husband, and children.

4. *What is the effect of making Miss Y a silent character? Of never bringing Mr. X (Bob) onstage at all? Of identifying the characters as "X" and "Y"?*

Calling the characters "X" and "Y" makes them seem like examples in a case study. They are the classic spurned wife and "other woman" in some senses. We do, in fact, know that Miss Y is named "Amelie," so the labels clearly have symbolic intent, suggesting that the characters' situations have a universal quality. Miss Y never speaks for herself, so we have only Mrs. X's analysis of the situation; we are left to infer how (or if) Miss Y would have defended herself. Mr. X remains a mystery; if we saw him, we would be able to tell how accurate his wife's analysis of the triangle really is. With Bob's remaining offstage, the audience is left with a wide range of speculations.

5. *What does the play's setting contribute toward its action and meaning? Explain why a more inclusive social setting in another time and place would be either more or less appropriate and effective than the setting Strindberg employs.*

The play is set in a cafe on Christmas Eve, a traditionally lonely time for the "other woman" in an affair. The setting emphasizes Miss Y's isolation and Mrs. X's cruelty in pursuing her relentless monologue about Miss Y and Mr. X. In a social situation with others present, we would have many points of view rather than the one point of view offered in this stark, isolated setting.

6. *Locate the places in the play where Miss Y is about to speak and where she responds with a facial expression or a bodily gesture. Explain how you would stage those moments.*

When Mrs. X enters, Miss Y simply looks up, nods, and resumes reading, indicating, perhaps, that she does not really want to engage in conversation. Very soon, Miss Y expresses disdain, then makes a gesture of fright (when the toy gun appears); and when Mrs. X discusses tulips, Miss Y "looks up from her magazine with an expression of irony mixed with curiosity." For a lively exercise, ask several groups of students to rehearse just these opening gestures and expressions (with two students playing the roles and at least one other in each group serving as director). Then have the groups present their interpretations, with the audience evaluating the different meanings suggested by the various interpretations of those playing Mrs. X and Miss Y.

Going Further

1. *Discuss the significance of the toy gun.*

2. *What do you think Mrs. X means when she says at the end of her second speech, ". . . you mean to say? . . . Ah, but there is a certain difference, don't you think?" What might Miss Y have implied by her look that would make Mrs. X respond in this way?*

3. *Imagine this play with Mrs. X as the silent character. Write several speeches for Miss Y, with stage directions indicating the gestures and reactions of Mrs. X.*

4. *Note the many references to slippers (along with the stage business). What is suggested about the husband's character by these references?*

5. *What is Mrs. X's profession? How does her profession relate to the action and characterization in the drama?*

A Marriage Proposal

Anton Chekhov (1860–1904)

Anton Chekhov's grandfather was a Russian serf who managed to buy freedom for himself, his wife, and his children. Chekhov's father, Pavel, became a shopkeeper but never forgot his difficult childhood. Unfortunately, he chose to practice the tyranny he had endured and acted as a despot to his wife and children. In addition to inflicting physical and mental abuse, Pavel Chekhov also insisted that his family follow the fanatic devotion to Orthodox religion that he himself practiced. Understandably, the Chekhov children resented the painful lack of freedom and grew up to despise all forms of oppression or unreasonable restraint. Along with his harsh home life, Anton Chekhov was given only a brief period of formal schooling (although he was a voracious reader and delighted in writing small dramas to be acted out by his brothers and himself). Before he was out of his childhood, like Ibsen and Strindberg before him, Anton Chekhov faced the exigencies of a bankrupt parent. Pavel, never the steadiest person, suffered business reverses, and betrayal by false friends caused him to move the family to a Moscow slum. Although Anton found the experience humiliating, it also provided his way out of his father's control. Known for his quick wit and intelligence, he tutored the nephew of a family acquaintance, thus earning his board and room while he completed enough schooling of his own to apply for (and win a scholarship for) five years of medical training.

During the years he pursued his medical degree, he began to write and publish short stories for the popular press, using his fees to eke out his meager stipend and to help support his still impoverished family. He turned out over a hundred stories each year (although he himself was the first to admit that their literary merit was highly questionable). He graduated as a doctor in 1884 and faced in the same year the grim irony that he was now a healer who had developed an incurable ailment, tuberculosis.

In spite of his illness, Chekhov continued to develop his literary talent, attributing his strict discipline to his scientific studies. He claimed medicine was his "lawful wife" while literature was his "mistress" (quoted by F. L. Lucas in *The Drama of Chekhov, Synge, Yeats and Pirandello,* Cassell, 1963). In 1890, Chekhov suddenly moved to an island east of Siberia to study convict life. The difficult journey and the observations he made of the penal colony at Sakhalin profoundly moved the young artist. Although he continued to appreciate the lighter sides of life that were the essence of his early plays and stories, he developed a keen sensitivity to the darker elements of human existence. His later plays demonstrate his sense of irony and questioning. The final years of his life were spent in the company of his beloved wife, Olga Knipper, who was also—quite appropriately—the leading lady in one of his plays. He died in 1904 of the tuberculosis that had haunted him for twenty years, calling on his deathbed for champagne and entertaining his heartbroken attendants with darkly humorous comments.

Teaching the Play

Students should be given assistance in understanding the complexities of Russian names. The character called Chubukov carries the full name Stepan Stepanovitch Chubukov and is respectfully addressed as "Stepan Stepanovitch" by his neighbor Lomov, whose full name is Ivan Vassilevitch Lomov. Chubukov's daughter, Natalia, is named Natalia Stepanovna Chubukova and is respectfully addressed by her first two names.

Summary of A Marriage Proposal

As the action begins, Lomov, who is dressed elegantly but displays great nervousness, calls on his older neighbor, the rich landowner Chubukov. Chubukov suspects his neighbor of wanting to borrow money and is overjoyed when he discovers that Lomov's true mission is to ask permission to marry Natalia, Chubukov's daughter. While the elated Chubukov summons his daughter, Lomov soliloquizes about his situation. He is 35 years old and feels that he must marry so that he might begin leading a "regular" life. By this he seems to mean overcoming his host of minor physical ailments, which each night prevent him from sleeping. He obviously has no great love for Natalia, and the most extravagant compliments he can bestow on her are that she is "not too bad looking" and that she has a good education. Natalia then enters, having been told by her father that "there's a merchant come to collect his goods." As the nervous Lomov begins to propose, Natalia and he get into a vigorous disagreement concerning ownership of a piece of land called the Oxen Meadows. Each claims ownership and offers absurdly complex arguments to back up the claim. As Natalia and Lomov become increasingly angry, with each shouting loud retorts to the other's statements, Chubukov returns and joins in the fray. He, of course, agrees with his daughter's claim of their family's ownership and summarily dismisses the Lomovs as "a pack of lunatics, the whole bunch of them!" The argument then degenerates to name-calling, and Lomov's response is to develop physical symptoms (a stitch in his side, a numb foot, etc.).

Lomov leaves, taking his symptoms with him, and both Natalia and Chubukov rail about his presumption until Chubukov reveals to his daughter that Lomov had intended to propose. Natalia then insists that Lomov be brought back and accuses her father of having ruined her chances to marry. When Lomov, still suffering symptoms, returns, Natalia assures him that the Oxen Meadows do indeed belong to him and that she had simply been mistaken. Natalia then tries to get Lomov back on the track of proposing, but before they exchange two sentences, the erstwhile lovers find themselves enmeshed in yet another argument, this time over who owns the best hunting dog. Chubukov is called upon to settle the argument, but, of course, he simply makes matters worse by challenging everything Lomov says. Lomov complains loudly about his terrible aches and pains while he, Chubukov, and Natalia shout the worst insults they can muster at each other. In the heat of battle, Lomov passes out and Natalia, believing he is dead, moans and groans about her loss. A quick drink of water revives him, however, and Chubukov greets the awakening younger man with the news that Natalia accepts his proposal. The bemused Lomov barely has time to express his joy when Natalia revives the dog argument. The play closes with the "happy" couple battling while the exasperated prospective father-in-law calls for champagne.

Discussion and Writing Topics

1. A Marriage Proposal is subtitled "A Joke in One Act." Identify and comment on the kinds and sources of humor in the play. What is the "joke" referred to in the subtitle?

There are many possible interpretations of the subtitle. Certainly each character has a "joke" played on him or her. Each desires the marriage for selfish reasons, imagining certain personal benefits, yet each will clearly face years of bickering, hypochondria, and dissatisfaction instead of the familial bliss, societal approval, and accumulation of wealth that are anticipated.

The play has many aspects of farce with its obvious, visual humor. We can see Lomov clutching his heart and stumbling around the stage making a picture as silly as that of Natalia dropping into a chair and screaming when she thinks the man she has been insulting unmercifully has dropped dead. Certainly the appearance, disappearance, and reappearance of Chubukov brings to mind slapstick comedy routines. In addition, the play is rich with irony. For instance, Natalia and Lomov each consider themselves superior beings, yet each shows willingness to accept a mate he or she believes to be inferior. As the audience watches the action unfold, it becomes clear, of course, that Natalia and Lomov richly deserve each other.

It is worth noting that although *A Marriage Proposal* is essentially a comedy, it offers a wise commentary on the perversity of human nature. Commenting on Chekhov's early plays, Eric Bentley in his preface to *The Brute and Other Farces* (Grove, 1958) notes:

> His greatest plays have a farcical component, and his slightest farces have something in them of the seriousness, pathos, and even subtlety of the greatest plays. . . . In its fine balance of contrasts—particularly of the pathetic and the ridiculous—a Chekhov farce might be regarded as a full-fledged Chekhov drama in miniature.

2. Why does Lomov decide to propose to Natalia? What are his reasons for wanting to get married, and what is your response to them?

Early in the play Lomov announces to the audience that he must get married because he is 35 years old and must now "settle down and lead a regular life." He attributes his many physical symptoms to his lack of a "regular life" and assumes that marrying will somehow make him both physically well and also, perhaps, more acceptable in a society that favors married couples more than carefree bachelors. As Lomov himself notes, he has no ideals when it comes to marriage, and he definitely is not in love with Natalia. In fact, the greatest compliment he can pay her is that she is an excellent housekeeper, followed by a comment that she is "not too bad looking" and that she has "had a good education."

Most students will be appalled that anyone would set out to marry for such pathetic reasons, but thoughtful readers will note that there is not such a very great distance between nineteenth-century Russia and America in the last decade of the twentieth century. People still stumble into marriage motivated by petty, selfish needs and without any real concern for what such a relationship should entail. The difference between Chekhov's play and our world, of course, is that on the stage such marriages can be viewed as comic; in real life they are almost always tragic.

3. Describe the structure of the plot and its relation to the proposed marriage.

The play divides neatly into two parts, each punctuated by an attempt at arranging a marriage proposal and ending in a trivial quarrel. In the first part, Lomov tries to get up his courage to ask Natalia for her hand but instead ends up in a spat about the ownership of the Oxen Meadows. He is driven away but called back, and the second part of the drama begins. Now it is Natalia who tries to encourage her suitor, but again, before the proposal can be made, the two start a debate about hunting dogs. The repetitive quarrels and the speed with which they occur make clear what the marriage will be like as does the fainting scene which comprises the climax and leads to the satirically comic resolution. The lovers will be united, yet the final scene is not the marriage dance of romantic comedy. We cannot, in our most farfetched dreams, imagine any of these characters "living happily ever after." Instead, they will be caught forever in drearily familiar squabbles. These three rather shallow people thrive on petty quarrels to keep their life interesting.

4. *Comment on the tempo of the play's action. Where is it slowest? Swiftest? What effect do these changes have?*

The pace slows when Lomov tries to explain himself either to Chubukov or to Natalia. (See, for instance, the opening exchange or the first conversation between Natalia and Lomov.) The slow pace suggests Lomov's phlegmatic nature and his tendency to avoid addressing issues directly. The tempo picks up considerably when Lomov inadvertently raises a point that irritates Natalia, escalating their discussion into a heated argument. The rapid exchanges and hasty exclamations indicate the problems the two will face if they persist in their determination to marry each other.

5. *Describe how you would stage the play. Identify possible problems that could develop in staging it, and explain how you would avoid or resolve them. Keep in mind the light mood of the play.*

One of the main problems with staging the play would involve the way Lomov portrays his various physical symptoms. If the audience thinks he really is having a heart attack, they will be concerned and fail to see the humor in Natalia's and Chubukov's reactions. Lomov's actions must be broad and comic so the audience clearly sees him for the buffoon he is.

Going Further

1. *Compare Molière's view of marriage in* The Doctor in Spite of Himself *with the view Chekhov presents in* A Marriage Proposal.

2. *What can you infer about the position of an unmarried woman in Russian society in the nineteenth century, considering Natalia's and Chubukov's reactions to Lomov's proposal?*

3. *What do the subjects of the quarrels suggest about the interests and values of the main characters?*

4. *Compare the father-daughter relationship in* An Enemy of the People *with the father-daughter relationship in* A Marriage Proposal.

5. *Write a scene showing Natalia, Chubukov, and Lomov at the wedding ceremony or on one of their anniversaries.*

Purgatory

William Butler Yeats (1865–1939)

William Butler Yeats was born into a creative family in Dublin, Ireland. Both his father and his brother were well-known artists, and his sister founded the Cuala Press, which published many works by Irish writers on national themes. As a child, Yeats was educated in London, but during his adolescent years he returned to his beloved Ireland, where he became fascinated by the folklore and tales of Irish storytellers. His first literary work was a long poem, *Mosada*, which was published in 1886. Later he became a founder of the Irish National Theatre Society (the Abbey Theatre) and began to write as well as produce plays that reflected nationalist themes. In addition to his brilliant writing, which won him the Nobel Prize for literature in 1923, Yeats was throughout his life an active national patriot. He worked tirelessly for the Irish Free State and promoted works of art and literature that revealed the Irish spirit.

Teaching the Play

Purgatory, written in 1938, the year before Yeats's death, reflects the dark vision of his maturity. In his introduction to *Yeats: A Collection of Critical Essays* (Prentice-Hall, 1963), John Unterecker asks where one might most profitably begin to read Yeats and answers his own question by noting that if a reader "is very wise, he will start with Yeats's poetry." Bearing this advice in mind, one might read some of the later poems, perhaps "The Second Coming" or "Sailing to Byzantium," as a prelude to considering *Purgatory.*

Summary of Purgatory

The play's two characters, called simply "Boy" and "Old Man," are revealed to be father and son. They contemplate the ruins of an old house while the father tells his son about the drama of that house. According to the Old Man, his father, a stable groom, had fallen in love with the daughter of the mansion's owner. In spite of her parents' protests, the girl married the stable groom and they lived together in her family home. The marriage turned out for the worse. The young wife died in childbirth; the husband squandered her fortune and (in what seems to be the most serious offense, according to the Old Man) he "killed the house." He destroyed the elegance and splendor of the house, making it mean and squalid. As a child, the Old Man was never educated because his father feared his son's growing above him, yet the village people who had loved his mother helped the young boy to read and write. The Boy, at this point, interrupts to point out that the Old Man gave *him* no education, but the Old Man brushes off the complaint as he thinks back to the night the house burned.

The Old Man admits he killed his father and left him to burn in the house. He had to flee because he was suspected and thus became a peddler. Now he claims to see a vision of the night his mother and father wed, the night he was conceived. The Old Man directly addresses his vision, pleading with his mother not to allow the act of love, to prevent his conception. As the vision fades, the Old Man accuses the Boy of rifling his pack looking for money. The two struggle for the bag, and the Old Man looks back at the window of the ruined house. This time both he and the Boy see the vision of a lighted window and a figure coming toward it. Suddenly, the Old Man turns and stabs the Boy, thus having killed his father and son "on the same jack-knife." He claims to have committed the murder to keep the Boy from growing up and passing on the "pollution" that he believes to be the consequence of his mother's unfortunate marriage. The play ends with the Old Man hearing again the hoofbeats that signal the beginning of the wedding night scenario, which he now realizes he is doomed to replay perpetually.

Discussion and Writing Topics

1. *Of what significance is the play's title? Is it apt? Why or why not?*

According to the Roman Catholic theology of Yeats's time, purgatory represented an intermediate state where souls who were not damned but who had not yet atoned for sins were allowed to expiate those sins. The Old Man tells us that "[t]he souls in Purgatory that come back . . . Re-live/ Their transgressions, and that not once/ But many times; they know at last/ The consequence of those transgressions/ Whether upon others or upon themselves."

These important lines suggest the significance of the title. The Old Man is not yet dead, yet he feels damned because he killed his father. He imagines that his mother must live and relive her wedding night because that, he believes, was the beginning of his own damnation. If his mother had not yielded to her lust and married a man who was not worthy of her in any way, he would not have been born and he would never have lived to act out the evil half (the half represented by his father) of his nature. The Old Man seeks to release his mother from her purgatory, but he perverts the traditional nature of expiation. Instead of seeking forgiveness for his act of patricide, he kills his son, rationalizing the murder as necessary to stamp out the evil in his father's line. The final scene reveals that the purgatory to be relived is as much his own as his mother's. He will never be able to stop seeing the trapped souls because his own is trapped in the same snare. Like the souls who "re-live their transgressions," he has returned to the scene of his original crime and has reenacted it by killing his son with the same knife.

2. What is the Old Man's attitude toward and relationship with the figures of his past, especially his father? Why are these figures important?

The Old Man feels ambivalent toward the mother he never knew in life. He has idealized her and sees her as beautiful and highborn. She lives in splendor, but then she betrays her nature by marrying the stable groom who comes drunk to the marriage bed and who squanders her fortune after her death. She is infatuated by her lust for the stableman and refuses to deny herself the sexual satisfaction for which she longs. The Old Man condemns his mother for what he considers the betrayal of her heritage.

Toward his father, the Old Man's feelings are far more clearly defined. He hates his father and always has. From the beginning, the Old Man has longed for the beauty and elegance of the mansion as it was before his mother's death, but his father has polluted all he touches and has "killed the house." The son longs for an education, but the father refuses to send him to school, fearing that the son will outdistance the father. When the mansion begins to burn in a fire the father starts in a drunken stupor, the son kills him, revenging in his own mind both the "death" of the house and the "death" of everything the house represents.

Both the mother and the father of the Old Man are important, for they represent to him the two sides of his nature. He believes that he has worthiness (from his mother) but that he also has the capacity for evil (from his father). As he sees the wedding night acted out over and over, he wishes to interfere and to prevent the cycle of his destruction. Ironically, his passion leads him to kill his own son, thus affirming (rather than purging) the evil side of his nature.

3. Identify and explain the play's theme or themes.

In "A Prayer for My Daughter," Yeats watches his sleeping child and wishes for her a husband who will "bring her to a house/ Where all's accustomed, ceremonious." He ends the poem with these lines:

> How but in custom and in ceremony
> Are innocence and beauty born?
> Ceremony's a name for the rich horn
> And custom for the spreading laurel tree.

The poem, then, praises what is beautiful, ordered, and traditional, just as does the play *Purgatory*. The daughter in the play chooses a bridegroom who not only does not bring her to a house "[w]here all's accustomed, ceremonious" but also disrupts and perverts the ancestral home in which she already lives. The play affirms the need to hold fast to old customs and to tradition. Disturbing the moral order (including the woman's yielding to what Yeats sees as her baser nature) can only bring disaster. One theme, then, might be that to challenge the established order is to wreak havoc. Another theme relates to the biblical observation that the sins of the fathers are visited on their children. The mother's initial yielding (symbolized by her bridal night of passion) condemns her not only to repeat the act over and over (with what pleasure, the Old Man wonders) but also to condemn her child and her grandchild to an unbreakable cycle of corruption and violence.

Although Yeats himself would probably have held with either of the readings suggested above, an alternative reading might question the play's point of view. Perhaps the Old Man is full of self-delusion. He blames all his problems on his mother's too hasty marriage and on his father's drunken brutality, yet he seems to ignore his own role. It is he who killed his father and then fled to lead the life of a rough peddler; it is he who decided not to educate his son (even though he resents bitterly his father's similar decision); and it is he who fails to share his wealth with his son. Although some scholars, like Peter Ure in *Yeats, The Playwright* (Barnes and Noble, 1963), see the Boy as "ignorant, amoral, thieving, a potential patricide, and—it is hinted—lecher," it is possible to see him as much more a victim than was his father. The Boy, after all, had none of the education, none of the advantages of the Old Man. Such a reading might reflect a theme of self-delusion.

The mother was deluded in thinking she was marrying a dashing prince. The Old Man was deluded in believing himself hopelessly caught in a web of fate; by doing nothing to escape that fate, but instead twice committing murder, he seals his doom.

4. *Explain the significance of the play's setting. What does it contribute to the tone, mood, and theme of the play?*

The setting is stark and dreamlike (or perhaps nightmarelike). The Boy and the Old Man stand before a ruined house with a bare tree in the background. It is night and the Old Man comments that "[t]he shadow of a cloud upon the house" is "symbolical." Everything indicates a mood of despair, sorrow, and inevitable tragedy. The tree is no longer fruitful, the cloud slides across the house, and the life that once inhabited the house has been wiped out or exiled to roam the earth, filled with bitterness, anger, and a lust for revenge.

5. *How does Yeats use speech and action to show the relationship between the Old Man and the Boy?*

When the Boy puts down his pack and stands in the doorway of the house, he literally puts himself in his father's place. Throughout the play, the Boy's speeches and actions reflect both his father's current thoughts and behaviors as well as the events of the Old Man's early life. The Boy is 16, the age at which the Old Man killed his father; the cycle seems doomed to repeat itself until the Old Man turns on the Boy with his knife, determined to stop the scene from replaying. (An intriguing biographical note: Yeats's son Michael was 16 when Yeats wrote this play!)

Going Further

1. *Discuss the significance of the tree. How does it symbolically suggest the changes in the Old Man's life?*

2. *What does the Old Man mean when he accuses his father of "killing the house"? Why does he declare the "murder" a capital offense? How might this view of "killing the house" justify the Old Man's later actions toward his father?*

3. *What age was the Old Man when his father burned down*

the house? What is the age of the Boy? What significance might there be in these statistics?

4. The Boy accuses the Old Man of being mad. What evidence is there to suggest that he is or is not crazy? Is the Boy sane? Explain your answer.

5. The Old Man condemns both his mother and his father. Create a scene in which the mother's spirit confronts the Old Man and explains her view.

Riders to the Sea

John Millington Synge (1871–1909)

Although John Millington Synge (pronounced "sing") wrote mainly about the rural Irish Catholic peasantry, he was born into a wealthy, Protestant, landholding family outside of Dublin. Synge made the connection with a world very different from his own through a series of circumstances and interests. First, because of his poor health, he was kept from school and grew up relatively isolated from peers who would have reinforced the values of the Protestant aristocracy. Separated from others his own age, he became an avid observer of the people and countryside around him. He learned to listen carefully and watch intently, often recording what he saw and heard in a journal. His isolation also led him to study on his own and he became fascinated with science. At 16, led by this interest, he read Darwin and then began to doubt and challenge the accepted religious beliefs of his family, taking a skeptical view toward dogmatic, organized religion. Another interest, also developed to fill the space left empty by his lack of companions, was music. Music provided the final bridge between Synge and the broad world that lay outside the narrow village in which he lived. He traveled to Germany, France, and Italy, learning and playing music with whomever he met. Yeats described him as "playing his fiddle to Italian sailors and listening to stories in the Bavarian mountains" (quoted by J. F. Lydon in his essay "John Millington Synge: The Man and His Background" in *Mosaic,* Spring 1971). When Synge returned from the continent, he became deeply interested in Irish politics and in the plight of Irish peasants. He, William Butler Yeats, and Lady Gregory (among others) founded the Abbey Theatre in Dublin, and he spent the rest of his short life (he died at 38) gathering materials for and writing his plays. He thought nothing of becoming a tramp, sleeping in ditches, and eating half-rotten food if it afforded him a chance to talk to the Irish men and women whose stories of the past mesmerized him and whose current living conditions moved him deeply. His plays, perhaps more than any others, bring the Irish peasantry—with all its virtues, flaws, foibles, strengths, and weaknesses—to the eyes of the world.

Teaching the Play

Although *Riders to the Sea* concerns rural Irish peasants in the nineteenth century, its theme is universal. Most students will know people whose lives are stunted by futilely repeated efforts. These people are caught in a cycle from which they could escape, yet they refuse to make the decisions necessary to free themselves from their self-defeating actions.

Summary of Riders to the Sea

Nora and her sister Cathleen talk about their mother's grief over the apparent drowning of their brother Michael. The sisters have received clothing removed from the body of a drowned man found many miles from where they live and have been asked by the parish priest to determine whether or not the clothing is Michael's. They hide the bundle when they hear their mother coming, thinking they will spare her until they know the news for certain. They then talk about their brother Bartley, who intends to sail to the horse market. When Bartley enters, Maurya, the mother, urges him not to go, but he insists that he must. He leaves without her blessing, but Nora and Cathleen urge her to catch up with him and bid him a proper farewell. As Maurya hurries away, her daughters take down the bundle and identify the clothes as Michael's. When their mother returns, they are astonished to hear her say she has seen not only Bartley but also Michael, who, she claims, was riding on the gray pony that Bartley led behind his own red mare. Maurya is terrified by her vision and believes it portends Bartley's death. At this point, we learn the depth of Maurya's tragedy: every man in her life has been drowned—her husband, her father-in-law, and so far five of her six sons. After their mother's outpouring of grief, Cathleen and Nora tell her that Michael's body has been found. Immediately, keening women fill the cottage, letting Maurya know that her worst fears have been fulfilled; Bartley, too, has drowned, having been knocked into the sea by the gray pony. Maurya's speeches create the powerful resolution of the play. She admits her losses and describes her gains. No longer will she worry and fret. The sea has taken from her all that it can. She has nothing to lose and so now can endure without constant anxiety.

Discussion and Writing Topics

1. To what extent can this play be described as a tragedy?

Certainly if we are using the standards of Aristotelian tragedy, *Riders* does not qualify completely. There is no character of high estate who falls from a position of power and happiness because of a tragic flaw. Still, the play has tragic elements. Certainly fate plays an important role. The young priest has assured Maurya that God will not take Bartley and leave her without a son to care for her. The sea, however, seems to operate outside the Christian framework. Steadily, inexorably, it has claimed every one of Maurya's male protectors. She cannot protect Bartley with her prayers and her worrying. The play's climax comes when Maurya sees the vision of Michael and recognizes her lack of control over the power of the sea. Once she admits this, she is able to reconcile herself to Bartley's death and to Michael's. As Thomas Kilroy suggests in his essay "Synge the Dramatist," she "attains tragic stature because [she] finds a freedom in isolation within [herself] . . . [she] attains a splendid isolation, self-containment, rising above the community of the play . . . with a contempt for the values that are left behind" (*Mosaic,* Spring 1971).

2. How would you describe the play's language—the speech style of the central characters? Of what importance is its religious dimension?

The characters speak in the dialect of Irish peasants. For example, Nora and Cathleen call Maurya "herself," giving her both affection and the respect due the oldest woman in the household. All the characters sprinkle their speech liberally with "God help us," or "The Son of God forgive us," or "The blessing of God on you." Still the Christian speech seems to be merely an external trapping, automatic phrases used superstitiously to ward off disaster. At the end of the play, Maurya acknowledges that her trips for holy water and her prayers have been for naught. She has been unable to win out against darker forces. We see hints of the supernatural in her vision of Michael, which portends both the news of his death and the drowning accident of Bartley. The sea (and perhaps, by implication, the old wrathful gods of natural forces) overpower the young priest's feeble assurances that "Almighty God won't leave her destitute with no son living."

3. Distinguish between the positions and roles of Nora and Cathleen.

Both daughters are concerned about their mother, but Cathleen, the elder, is sharper and takes her mother to task. For instance, when Maurya allows Bartley to go off to market without her blessing, it is Cathleen who scolds her and urges her to catch up with him. Cathleen also takes charge more than Nora does. The older sister hides the bundle of clothes and later directs the examination of the garments and then urges that the sad evidence be hidden from Maurya until Bartley returns from his voyage. When Maurya returns and tells of her astonishing vision, Cathleen gently insists that she could not have seen Michael because he is dead. As the play closes, Cathleen is once again taking charge of the family concerns. She asks the men to make a coffin and explains to Nora (who thinks her mother's lack of tears at Bartley's death means she loved Michael better) that Maurya is old and that she has exhausted herself with the depth of her weeping for the nine days since Michael was reported drowned.

4. What is Maurya's role? Describe in general terms the kind of actress you imagine would be well suited to her role.

Maurya is the play's protagonist, an old woman who has suffered greatly and who comes to an epiphany of grief at the end of the play. She recognizes that she can now let go of all her worrying and fearing. She has experienced her worst nightmare and nothing else can touch her. The actress who plays Maurya must be able to depict a simple peasant woman convincingly for the earlier scenes with Nora and Cathleen when she scolds and goads them and for her scene with Bartley when she tries to convince him not to go to sea. But she must also be able to project an existential transcendence in her moving final speech. Students may enjoy naming actresses who might be recruited for the role. Colleen Dewhurst comes to mind, for example.

5. *Identify the props used and comment on their dramatic and symbolic significance.*

The nets and oilskins that hang on the kitchen walls suggest that the sea and its related occupations are an integral part not only of the men who work at sea but also of the women who wait for them in the cottage. Cathleen sits at the spinning wheel as the play opens, suggesting the spinning wheel of fate that pulls together, inevitably, the threads of human lives. The boards, we learn, have been purchased for Michael's coffin. The sea, fate, and death, then, are the central residents of the cottage kitchen. Other props include Michael's clothes, the rope (intended to lower Michael into his grave, but taken by Bartley to lead his horse), the shawl Maurya puts over her head, and the bread Maurya takes to Bartley (an intended communion that ends as last rites).

6. *Explain the significance of the title. How does Synge make the presence and the power of the sea felt without ever "showing" it to us directly?*

Bartley is, of course, a literal "rider to the sea," but the title clearly implies a great deal more. All the men in Maurya's life have been drawn to (or forced to) the sea to make a living. In spite of the terrible dangers and the losses they face, these men move (ride) through their lives knowing that, at the end, the sea will claim them. As is discussed in question 5 (above), the props of the play show the domination of the sea, as do the dialogue and actions of the characters as they ask each other about the condition of the sea, go to the window to watch the approach of the ships, and so on.

Going Further

1. *Why is the information concerning the deaths of Maurya's husband, father-in-law, and first four sons withheld until near the end of the play? How would the play be changed if the audience knew about these losses from the beginning?*

2. *What are we to make of Maurya's vision of Michael? Does she really see a ghost? Does she imagine him? Why is he described as wearing new shoes?*

3. *Note how Cathleen and Nora react to their brother's clothes as they examine them. Do you find this scene convincing?*

4. *What is the significance of the comments made by the men who come to the cottage after Bartley's death? How do they compare or contrast with Maurya's speeches?*

Trifles

Susan Glaspell (1882–1948)

Born in Davenport, Iowa, Susan Glaspell was the daughter of a feed dealer and an Irish immigrant. She spent her early years in Davenport, where she had the opportunity to observe the rural characters who appear in many of her writings. Following her graduation from Drake University in 1899, she worked as a reporter for the *Des Moines Daily News*. Her early short stories and novels, many of which were written while she worked for the *Daily News,* are considered fine examples of regionalist literature. When she began to earn enough money from her creative writing to support herself, Glaspell moved to Greenwich Village, New York, in

1911. In 1913, she married George Cram Cook, ironically a "home town boy" who also came from Davenport, Iowa. The two spent winters in Greenwich Village, where Glaspell wrote and Cook directed plays. They helped to found the Playwrights' Theater there. Summers were devoted to the Provincetown Players, a theatrical group founded by Cook and Glaspell at their summer residence on Cape Cod in Massachusetts. At both theaters, actors performed Glaspell's plays as well as plays by such renowned playwrights as Eugene O'Neill and Edna St. Vincent Millay. Both theaters took daring risks, presenting avant-garde drama with little concern for financial success. In fact, ironically, when their ventures began to show a profit, Cook lost interest; and he and Glaspell became expatriates in Greece, where they lived from 1922 until 1924, when Cook died. Glaspell remarried briefly (from 1925–1931) and spent the remaining years of her life in Provincetown, writing. During her life, Glaspell published ten novels and more than forty short stories, and in 1930 she won the Pulitzer Prize for drama with *Alison's House,* a dramatization of the life of a poet, said to be based on Emily Dickinson.

Teaching the Play

Although *Trifles* was published in 1916, its theme is remarkably timely. The characters play out the traditional roles assigned to men and women, yet the ironic ending issues a strong challenge to those stereotypes.

Glaspell was living the life of an emancipated career woman in the city when she wrote this play, but the characters in *Trifles* who assert the right for women to be respected and to lead productive, dignified lives are not big-city professionals or social rebels. Instead, they are simple farm women who nevertheless understand their fundamental rights as human beings.

Summary of Trifles

The County Attorney, George Henderson, and the Sheriff, Henry Peters, come into the kitchen of the now-abandoned farmhouse of John and Minnie Wright. They are investigating a murder and have brought with them Mrs. Peters and Mr. and Mrs. Hale, neighbors of the Wrights. Henderson questions and challenges the Sheriff about the condition of the house, wondering if everything has been left as it was found. Henry Peters brushes off the questions with defensive explanations about his busy life as a lawman. Lewis Hale then tells his story of finding John Wright's body. He had gone to the farm to propose installing a telephone line, but instead found Mrs. Wright rhythmically rocking in her chair, looking "kind of done up." She told Hale he couldn't see John because he was dead. Lewis and his friend Harry, who had come with him to propose the telephone line, then went to the bedroom and saw that Mrs. Wright had been telling the truth when she said her husband "died of a rope round his neck." She explained that someone came in and choked him while she was asleep. After listening to Hale's explanation, the lawmen begin to look around a little, and the County Attorney accidentally dirties his hands with some fruit from jars that have frozen and exploded. Mrs. Peters says Mrs. Wright had been worried about that happening, which brings guffaws from the men, who believe that it's typical of women to be "worrying over trifles," even when something important like murder is at hand. The men decide to inspect the bedroom, but before they go, the County Attorney makes several disparaging remarks about Minnie Wright's housekeeping. Mrs. Hale defends Minnie to Mrs. Peters, but Mrs. Peters notes that it's the duty of the men to observe such things.

As they continue to discuss the case, Mrs. Peters notes that the lawmen suspect Mrs. Wright, but need to find a motive. The men return and once again make fun of the women for noticing little things, like Minnie's quilting materials. After the men leave to inspect the barn, the two women find a quilt square that has terribly odd, uneven sewing. Mrs. Hale pulls out the stitches, although Mrs. Peters is nervous about her doing that. When the two women look in Minnie's sewing basket to see if they can find things for her to occupy herself with while she is being held in jail for investigation, they discover the body of a bird with its neck broken. They then surmise that Minnie had the bird as her only company and only comfort from her harsh, taciturn husband. They imagine that John Wright, who hated any conversation or noise, must have tired of the bird's singing and killed it. This scenario, of course, would provide a motive for the murder. When the men return, the women have to make a decision. Although Mrs. Peters's loyalties are torn, when the County Attorney condescendingly notes that she is "married to the law," she seems to make her decision. Along with Mrs. Hale, she tacitly agrees to suppress the evidence. She starts to pick up the box with the bird, and when she cannot, Mrs. Hale puts it into the large pocket of her coat. The men continue to laugh at the women's attention to detail, but Mrs. Hale has the final speech—and the final, grim laugh.

Discussion and Writing Topics

1. Explain the significance of the title. Do you prefer this title or the one Glaspell gave her rewriting of the play as a short story, "A Jury of Her Peers"?

The men in Glaspell's play assume that women's work is trivial, far less important than their work. Note the exchange over the fruit, which ends with Lewis Hale commenting that "women are used to worrying over trifles." Of course, it is just such "trifles" that lead Mrs. Hale and Mrs. Peters to find the motive for the murder that the men, with their self-important posturing, fail to discover. For example, the men condemn Mrs. Wright because she doesn't have clean towels. When it offends their sensibilities, the men are ready to place blame for what women have failed to do, but they do not bother to ask themselves what the situation might have been. Mrs. Hale and Mrs. Peters, on the other hand, are not so quick to judge their neighbor, but wonder instead if one of the Sheriff's men might have soiled the towel. The women notice the "trifles" that make the work load in their lives unnecessarily heavier and question why things are that way, whereas the men, because they feel they have not been properly "taken care of" as they tear apart her house looking for a motive for murder, casually criticize the imprisoned Mrs. Wright's housekeeping skills. They are more interested in a clean towel for their own hands than they are in trying to understand Mrs. Wright—for whatever reasons, judicial or humane.

Students' responses will differ regarding the title of the work. Certainly "A Jury of Her Peers" suggests the discrepancies in a system of justice where (especially in 1916, when this play was

written) the power rests primarily in the hands of men. Mrs. Hale
and Mrs. Peters "try" Mrs. Wright and find her innocent on the
grounds of justifiable homicide. Given the evidence of the broken-
necked bird, a male jury might well have made a different decision.

2. *Explain the irony in the final line of the play. How does Mrs.
Hale's response to the County Attorney reflect the moral dilemma
she and Mrs. Peters have been facing?*

The wonderful pun on "knot it" ("not it") sums up the irony in
the play. The men condescendingly ask about the women's term
for working a quilt, but in her response Mrs. Hale reflects the
resolution to the conflict she and Mrs. Peters have been facing.
They have discovered what they assume (with good reason) to be
the cruel work of Mr. Wright and thus could offer to the Sheriff
the important motive that he lacks for understanding the crime
and the particular way in which it was committed. In analyzing
the crime, however, the women have discovered the situation to
be more complex than they had imagined. Mrs. Peters agonizes
over whether to tell her husband, but perhaps she resents being
described as "married to the law," or perhaps the scales are tipped
by the condescending question of the County Attorney. At any
rate, Mrs. Hale firmly announces the jury's verdict when she says,
"We call it—knot it, Mr. Henderson." The men have *not* discovered *it* (the motive) because they are unable to understand the truth
of Mrs. Wright's life, and by extension the lives of all women. The
women, having found the motive acceptable, will *not* reveal *it*. In
their judgment, Mrs. Wright is *not it,* not guilty.

3. *How does Glaspell enlist our sympathy for the women? How
do Mrs. Hale and Mrs. Peters get along with each other and with
the men?*

Although Mrs. Peters is more reluctant than Mrs. Hale to excuse
Minnie Wright, she is willing to hear what Mrs. Hale has to say.
As the two discover the evidence together, they also discuss ex-
periences that were typical, especially in their day, for women.
Mrs. Hale describes Minnie's pleasure in singing in the choir when
she was a young girl and her loss of joy once she was married to
John Wright, her inability even to belong to the Ladies Aid Society
because of his penury. When Mrs. Hale and Mrs. Peters discover

the canary and speculate on what its loss must have meant to Minnie, Mrs. Peters says, "I know what stillness is." And she recalls the loss of her first child during the years she and her husband were homesteading. Mrs. Peters also remembers her feelings when her childhood pet, a kitten, had been deliberately killed by a bully. The women talk together, opening up their lives and their emotions, as they gather items for Minnie. Although Minnie is not physically present, Mrs. Hale and Mrs. Peters form a community with her, a community from which the men are excluded primarily because they choose not to enter. The men condescend to the women and treat them with jocular teasing. The women never overtly challenge the men or question their comments, but in the end Mrs. Hale and Mrs. Peters hold the power. They could provide the Sheriff with his motive, but they choose to close ranks around their fellow woman and to protect a person they have come to regard as a brutally wounded bird.

4. *How does Glaspell characterize each of the three men in the play—the County Attorney, the Sheriff, and the neighboring farmer? What attitudes toward women do the men display? Support your answer with examples.*

The County Attorney is officious and self-important. He patronizes the women (for example, inviting them up to the fire as though the house were his rather than the Wrights'). Mr. Hale is impressed with the murder investigation and shows himself to be a rather simple man who is none too brave (he wanted his friend to go upstairs with him once Minnie had told him her husband was dead). He shows his attitude toward women when he admits that he was going to appeal to Minnie to get a party telephone line put in. He clearly thinks that, as a woman, she would favor the idea of having a telephone that would provide communication with her neighbors. Hale also is the character who notes that "women are used to worrying over trifles"; ironically, in his speeches he shows that he, in fact, is caught up with the trivia of life. The Sheriff is busy defending himself and his methods to the County Attorney. He looks hurriedly in the room and pronounces, "Nothing here but kitchen things." Yet it is among the "kitchen things" that the women eventually find the evidence that none of the men can discover.

5. *Which of the stage props are most important for the dramatic action of the play? For its theme? Explain your answer.*

Certainly the empty birdcage and the sewing box with the dead bird are the most important props. The birdcage suggests the trap Minnie found herself in when she married the dour John Wright, while the bird, apparently killed by the man who could not bear to hear a cheerful sound, symbolizes Minnie herself and also explains her choice of murder method. The quilt, too, is important. It represents the "trifles" of women's work that become so significant in the play; and, in addition, when Mrs. Hale at the end answers the County Attorney's facetious question by firmly responding, "We call it—knot it," we can imagine Mrs. Wright knotting not only her quilt but also the noose that strangled her husband.

6. *Explain how you might stage this play to convey its tension.*

Answers will vary widely, but certainly the men must swagger around and take up most of center stage when they are present, showing their importance and their dismissal of the women, who should stand in the background or to the side. When the women are together, they should take center stage so that their world now becomes prominent. There is tension also between Mrs. Peters and Mrs. Hale, and the staging might indicate this by having them move toward or away from each other (or face toward or away from each other) as each struggles with her growing knowledge of Minnie's role in her husband's death.

Going Further

1. *At what point in reading* Trifles *did you realize that Mrs. Wright had murdered her husband?*

2. *What is the central conflict in the drama? Is there more than one important conflict? Are the conflicts resolved? How?*

3. *Describe the married life of the Wrights as suggested by Mrs. Hale's comments and by other evidence in the play.*

4. *What role is played by the setting in this play? How does the setting reveal character and suggest the theme of the play?*

5. What is the effect of the play's chronology? Why would Glaspell choose to present the murder offstage and simply show the investigation? Would the play's theme be different if, instead, she showed the steps leading up to the murder first and then the murder as the play's climax? Explain your answer.

The Glass Menagerie

Tennessee Williams (1911–1983)

Tennessee Williams, born Thomas Lanier Williams, was the son of a traveling shoe salesman who prided himself on his years as a lieutenant in the Spanish-American War and on his ancestry of rugged frontiersmen and Indian fighters. His mother had been raised gently as the daughter of an Episcopal clergyman and cherished a romantic view of the antebellum South, with its gracious social life and elegant plantations. Williams was born in Mississippi because his father's occupation kept him away from the family, and thus his mother chose to return to the sheltered, dependable cocoon of the Episcopal rectory. Williams spent his early years there, a favorite of his grandfather, who read to him, told him stories, and recited exciting narrative poetry that delighted the young boy.

In 1918 the family moved to St. Louis to be with Cornelius Williams. The move was most unhappy for Thomas. His father tried to get him interested in sports and found his son's interest in reading a "womanish" trait. Tom hated the shabby apartment they were forced to live in because Cornelius never adequately supported the family. *The Glass Menagerie* reflects, to a modest degree, Williams's home life as a young man during his years in St. Louis. His sister, though shy, was not physically incapacitated and did not collect glass figures. His father evidently did not abandon the family, though he did have a drinking problem. And like Tom Wingfield, the young Tennessee Williams was unhappy at work and sought fulfillment in attending movies, writing poetry, and finally in wandering.

A gift of a ten-dollar typewriter from his mother on his twelfth birthday started Williams on his writing career. When he was still in high school, he began to earn money with his fiction, receiving $35 from the magazine *Weird Tales* for his story "The Vengeance of Nitocris." When he finished high school, Williams entered the University of Missouri, where he became a journalism major. After two years, however, his grades were so poor that his father forced him to drop out of school and take a job in the same shoe factory where he was employed. Two years later, suffering from physical and mental exhaustion, Williams left and moved in with his grandparents, who now lived in Memphis. During his stay with them he developed an interest in drama, and when he returned to St. Louis, he joined a small theatrical group called The Mummers. Although Williams continued to develop his talent in writing drama, his career was set back by his sister Rose's mental illness. In 1937 she was committed to an insane asylum, and Williams was deeply distressed by his inability to help her and by the loss of the family member to whom he had felt closest.

After several failed attempts, Williams completed college and earned his B.A. from the University of Iowa. He refused to go back to work in the shoe factory, so he broke his family ties and moved to New Orleans, adopting as his pen name "Tennessee," the label given him by his college classmates. Working at odd jobs to support himself, Williams got his first break when a one-act play won a $100 contest and an agent who liked the play got Williams a grant to continue his writing. *The Glass Menagerie,* which opened in 1945, was his first solidly successful play, followed by *A Streetcar Named Desire,* for which he won the Pulitzer Prize in 1947. Other well-known dramas by Williams include *Summer and Smoke* (1948), *The Rose Tattoo* (1951), *Cat on a Hot Tin Roof* (1955), and *Suddenly Last Summer* (1958).

Teaching the Play

These are Williams's own production notes about how to stage *The Glass Menagerie:*

Being a "memory play," *The Glass Menagerie* can be presented with unusual freedom of convention. Because of its considerably delicate or tenuous material, atmospheric touches and subtleties of direction play a particularly important part. Expressionism and all other unconventional techniques in drama have only one valid aim, and that is a closer approach to truth. When a play employs unconventional techniques, it is not, or certainly shouldn't be, trying to escape its responsibility of dealing with reality, or interpreting experience, but is actually or should be attempting to find a closer approach, a more penetrating and vivid expression of things as they are. The straight realistic play with its genuine Frigidaire and authentic ice-cubes, its characters that speak exactly at its audience speaks, corresponds to the academic landscape and has the same virtue of a photographic likeness. Everyone should know nowadays the unimportance of the photographic in art: that truth, life, or reality is an organic thing which the poetic imagination can represent or suggest, in essence, only through transformation, through changing into other forms than those which were merely present in appearance.

These remarks are not meant as a preface only to this particular play. They have to do with a conception of a new, plastic theater which must take the place of the exhausted theater of realistic conventions if the theater is to resume vitality as a part of our culture.

The Screen Device.   There is *only one important difference between the original and acting version of the play* and that is the *omission* in the latter of the device which I tentatively included in my *original* script. This device was the use of a screen on which were projected magic-lantern slides bearing images or titles. I do not regret the omission of this device from the present Broadway production. The extraordinary power of [Laurette] Taylor's performance made it suitable to have the utmost simplicity in the physical production. But I think it may be interesting to some readers to see how this device was conceived. So I am putting it into the published manuscript. These images and legends, projected from behind, were cast on a section of wall between the front-room and dining-room areas, which should be indistinguishable from the rest when not in use.

The purpose of this will probably be apparent. It is to give accent to certain values in each scene. Each scene contains a particular point (or several) which is structurally the most important. In an episodic play, such as this, the basic structure or narrative line may be obscured from the audience; the effect may seem fragmentary rather than architectural. This may not be the fault of the play so much as a lack of attention in the audience. The legend or image upon the screen will strengthen the effect of what is merely allusion in the writing and allow the primary point to be made more simply and lightly than if the entire responsibility were on the spoken lines. Aside from this structural value, I think the screen will have a definite emotional appeal, less definable but just as important. An imaginative producer or director may invent many other uses for this device than those indicated in the present script. In fact the possibilities of the device seem much larger to me than the instance of this play can possibly utilize.

The Music   Another extra-literary accent in this play is provided by the use of music. A single recurring tune, "The Glass Menagerie," is used to give emotional emphasis to suitable passages. This tune is like circus music, not when you are on the grounds or in the immediate vicinity of the parade, but when you are at some distance and very likely thinking of something else. It seems under those circumstances to continue almost interminably and it weaves in and out of your preoccupied consciousness; then it is the lightest, most delicate music in the world and perhaps the saddest. It expresses the surface vivacity of life with the underlying strain of immutable and inexpressible sorrow. When you look at a piece of delicately spun glass you think of two things: how beautiful it is and how easily it can be broken. Both of those ideas should be woven into the recurring tune, which dips in and out of the play as if it were carried on a wind that changes. It serves as a thread of connection and allusion between the narrator with his separate point in time and space and the subject of his story. Between each episode it returns as reference to the emotion, nostalgia, which is the first condition of the play. It is primarily Laura's music and therefore comes out most clearly when the play focuses upon her and the lovely fragility of glass which is her image.

The Lighting   The lighting in the play is not realistic. In keeping with the atmosphere of memory, the stage is dim. Shafts of light are focused on selected areas or actors, sometimes in contradistinction to what is the apparent center. For instance, in the quarrel scene between Tom and Amanda, in which Laura has no active part, the clearest pool of light is on her figure. This is also true of the supper scene, when her silent figure on the sofa should remain the visual center. The light upon Laura should be distinct from the others, having a peculiar pristine clarity such as light used in early religious portraits of female saints or madonnas. A certain correspondence to light in religious paintings, such as El Greco's, where the figures are radiant in atmosphere that is relatively dusky, could be effectively used throughout the play. (It will also permit a more effective use of the screen.) A free, imaginative use of light can be of enormous value in giving a mobile, plastic quality to plays of a more or less static nature.

Summary of The Glass Menagerie

Scene I   The first scene opens with the narrator, Tom Wingfield, giving a retrospective view of his family's apartment as it appeared during the Depression years, when the world was filled with the threat of foreign wars, labor problems, and a severely depressed economy. Tom introduces the audience to his mother, Amanda, and his sister, Laura, and refers to a "gentleman caller." His father appears only as a picture on the wall. It is clear from the beginning that Tom and his mother do not get along. She harasses him about the way he eats and complains about his smoking. When she leaves Tom alone, she begins reminiscing about the elegant days of her youth when gentleman callers filled the house and insists that Laura keep herself nicely dressed in anticipation of her own gentleman callers.

Scene II   Laura is arranging her glass animals, but hurries to her typewriter when her mother enters. Amanda, with some melodrama, confronts Laura with dropping out of business school and hiding her action. Laura admits she was unable to cope and threw up when faced with the first speed test. As Amanda and Laura talk, Laura reveals that she was once interested in a boy in high school, Jim, who teasingly called her "Blue Roses" because that is how he heard "pleurosis," a disease she was suffering from.

Scene III   Amanda decides to find a gentleman caller for Laura. Next, Tom and Amanda clash, with Tom accusing her of meddling in his life and telling her how much he loathes his work in a factory warehouse. He ends by calling his mother a "babbling old witch," and starts to storm out of the apartment. On his way, he accidentally breaks some of Laura's glass animals; and when he hears his sister cry out, he stops and walks slowly toward her, miserable over what he has done.

Scene IV   Tom returns to the apartment, obviously drunk, after spending the evening watching an all-night movie and what he claims was a magic show. Laura gently puts Tom to bed while the portrait of their father is illuminated to dominate the scene symbolically. The next morning, after Laura leaves to shop, Amanda and Tom confront each other. Each expresses both grievances and regrets, and when Amanda confides her fears about Laura never gaining independence from the family by finding a husband, Tom reluctantly agrees to invite a friend home for dinner.

Scene V   Tom appears again in the role of narrator and comments on the social and historical events that were occurring during the time of the play's action. Amanda's voice calls Tom back to the world of the apartment. As he sits on the fire escape talking to his mother, he tells her that he has invited Jim O'Connor, a friend of his, home to dinner. Amanda excitedly makes plans, although Tom cautions her that Jim and Laura are very different and that Laura cannot be expected to play the role of a social deb. Amanda ignores him and calls to Laura, telling her to look at the moon and make a wish.

Scene VI   Tom is once again the narrator. The frequent shifts to the older Tom emphasize the idea that the play takes place entirely in Tom's memory and that the scenes are remembered as fragments rather than actual events. Tom provides information about Jim, noting that he and Laura were in high school together. He does not realize, however, that Laura has had a crush on Jim for years.

Amanda goes through elaborate preparations, and when the door-bell sounds, she pushes forward the panicky Laura (who has heard Jim's name and now knows who is expected). Laura opens the door, then rushes off, embarrassed, and later, when her mother insists that she sit at the dinner table, becomes ill and must be excused. Amanda plays the role of the Southern belle, but her charm cannot cover the awkwardness of Laura's misery.

Scene VII After dinner, the lights suddenly go out (because Tom has taken the money intended to pay the bill and used it to pay dues to the Union of Merchant Seamen, which he has secretly joined). To punish Tom, Amanda insists that he help with the dishes and drags him off to the kitchen, giving Jim the chance to be alone with Laura. Jim picks up a candelabrum and walks into the living room, where Laura sits up nervously. Jim's gentle and unpretentious talking boosts Laura's confidence, and she tells him about their high school connection. At first Jim doesn't remember, but when Laura reminds him about the nickname "Blue Roses," he recalls seeing her. Laura describes how shy she was and how painfully self-conscious she was about her limp. Jim reassures her and describes his own trials since leaving high school. He has over-come his own feeling of inferiority by becoming interested in a career in radio engineering. Laura counters by telling of her interest in her glass collection. The two "interests" are so very different — one leading out into the world, one maintaining a fantasy world — that readers/viewers can tell Jim and Laura are not soul mates. Nevertheless, the dinner, the wine, and the candlelight cast a cer-tain spell. Laura tells Jim about her favorite glass animal, the tiny unicorn. As Laura replaces the glass unicorn on the table, music from the Paradise Dance Hall across the alley comes through the window and Jim asks her to dance. She is literally swept off her feet as the enthusiastic and warmhearted Jim twirls her around. As they dance, they bump into the table. The unicorn falls and its horn breaks off. Laura says it no longer matters; the unicorn now can be happy to be just like the rest of the horses.

Laura seems changed; she recognizes that she no longer needs to be different or to think herself different. Jim reacts to the change with compliments, reassurances, and a kiss. But at the moment of the kiss, Jim suddenly realizes he has gone too far. He hastily apologizes and tells Laura about his fiancée, Betty. Laura listens silently as Jim tells her that when Tom invited him to dinner, he had not realized Tom had a sister. When he begs her to speak, she gives him the broken unicorn as a souvenir of the evening. Amanda then enters, bearing lemonade and urging that all drink to "[t]he gaiety of the occasion." After a somber toast, Jim announces that he must leave, and when Amanda invites him to call whenever he likes, he explains about his engagement. Although Amanda remains gracious to Jim, as soon as the door closes, she turns to Tom, berating him for not knowing that his best friend was engaged. Tom heads for the door and, when Amanda questions him, announces that he is going "to the movies"; we sense, however, that he, too, like his father, will leave Amanda behind. Amanda accuses Tom of being a "selfish dreamer," and the scene ends with Amanda silently comforting her daughter, who sits at the end of the sofa.

As the scene ends, Tom reenters as the narrator and describes his escape from St. Louis and his travels. He tried to forget his sister, but something—perhaps a line of music or a piece of transparent glass—would bring the painful memories of her back to him. He asks that Laura help him now to erase these haunting images. As he urges her, "Blow out your candles, Laura," his sister (or perhaps we can say the memory of Laura) leans forward and blows out the flames on the candelabrum.

Discussion and Writing Topics

1. The Glass Menagerie is arranged as a sequence of seven scenes. Explain how the scenes are related.

The scenes are tied together by the play's major themes. For example, the Wingfields are all isolated and lonely, each in his or her own way. Each has a way of escaping, Amanda by dreaming of past splendor, Tom by drinking and going to the movies, and Laura by staying at home and immersing herself in the world of her glass animal collection. Themes to consider, then, include isolation, loneliness, escape, and fantasy versus reality.

The scenes are also tied together, of course, by the action of the two plots: Tom's plans to leave the family and join the merchant marine and Amanda's plans to find a husband for Laura. Every scene in some way reveals the hostility and anger Tom feels about his living and working situation, just as every scene shows something about Laura's special nature and the bleak prospects she faces in life.

2. Why does Williams employ a narrator in this play? How would you characterize his role? What would be gained or lost without the narrator?

Without the narrator, the play would be entirely changed. Because of the narrator, we see the action as memory, and it takes on the hazy, mythic qualities of all memories. We cannot be sure what actually happened and what the narrator simply thinks happened. Like memories, the scenes in the play are selective. We remember what we want to remember or what we are forced to remember. Tom is trapped by his memories. He cannot help replaying some scenes over and over again, and that is what we are shown in the play. Also, as an older narrator, Tom can provide for us the social context of the play. We realize that as the war in the Wingfield household is being played out, the world outside that seems lively, spirited, and music-filled is, in fact, preparing itself for a devastating war. The ironies of the setting would be lost if we had no narrator to place the main action of the play in a larger context. The narrator acts as a guide and interpreter for the reader/viewer, remaining largely outside the action until the end of the play. Then he seems to speak directly to the remembered Laura, urging her to blow out her candles, to erase herself from his memory (or at least to purge the pain from his memory). Since Laura complies, leaning forward and extinguishing the flames on the candelabrum, we can reasonably speculate that the play provides a catharsis for Tom, who has now told his sister's story and can be free from its agony.

3. Explain the value to Laura and the meaning for us of her collection of glass animals. Don't overlook the unicorn.

Laura's collection represents her fantasy world. When Jim talks about the importance of having an interest so that one keeps motivated, he uses as an example his fascination with radio engineering. Laura, however, can offer only her collection as an interest, and it is an activity that draws her further away from the world rather than into the world (as does Jim's practical interest). The figures in the menagerie are beautiful and fragile, like Laura herself. They are also, however, frozen, cold, and locked forever in one form. Laura shares these qualities, too. She is unable to cope with normal pressures and situations and so keeps her feelings and fears locked up inside. Like the glass animals, she can never grow and mature emotionally.

The unicorn, of course, is Laura's favorite animal and it most closely resembles her. It is different from all the other horses because it has a horn. Jim notes that unicorns are extinct in the modern world, and, indeed, Laura herself seems to have escaped from some far earlier time when princesses could stay sheltered and locked up in protected towers. When Laura and Jim dance, the horn is broken from the unicorn. It becomes like the rest of the horses, and Laura seems to recognize that such a move toward the ordinary may, in fact, be positive. When Jim reveals that he is engaged, however, she loses the tiny thread of confidence she had gained and slips back into her glass world. The unicorn must go with Jim because it carries memories of Laura's one special moment and, perhaps, also because it no longer belongs entirely to the fantasy world where Laura will once again retreat.

4. Besides the glass animals, what other objects assume symbolic significance? What do they represent?

Possibilities abound. Here are some suggestions:

Blue Roses: Jim's nickname for Laura suggests once again an unreal, fantasy beauty. Jim innocently transforms the name of an ugly disease into a lovely phrase. For Laura, it represents a cherished memory and the possibility of love. For Jim, it represents misunderstanding, which is central to his relationship with Laura.

Blue Mountain: Blue is also significant in Amanda's life. But her "blue" is a remembered place rather than a name. She thinks of her childhood and young girlhood, and for her it represents a time when she was beautiful and desired. She idealizes Blue Mountain and compares her situation there with her current circumstances. In one sense, Blue Mountain sustains her, but in another it prevents her from facing the reality of her daughter's desperate isolation.

The Picture of Mr. Wingfield: In the opening dialogue, Tom introduces his father as "a fifth character." Mr. Wingfield never appears in the play, yet his picture is illuminated at significant moments. For instance, in Scene IV the light glows on the portrait as Tom drunkenly complains to Laura about the confinement of his life. The father's influence over the family is evident throughout the play. Amanda never stops moaning about her wretched choice of husband, yet she advises her son to improve his grooming habits, noting that attention to personal appearance was the one thing his father had plenty of. And, of course, Mr. Wingfield's bolting from the family foreshadows Tom's own escape at the end of the play.

5. *Look carefully at the stage description for the first scene. Single out three features of that description and comment on their significance.*

The dark walls of the tenement in which the Wingfields live and the darker alleys that surround it suggest the darkness and depression of the family's life. In addition, the tenement seems to be a trap, with the fire escape, where Tom often sits, as the only means of getting free. The transparent fourth wall of the building and the transparent gauze portieres give the scene a hazy, blurred look that suggests the quality of memory. The setting definitely reflects Tom's claim that "[t]he play is memory. Being a memory play, it is dimly lighted, it is sentimental, it is not realistic."

6. *Explain the function and significance of the interpolated "legends." What would be gained or lost without them?*

Williams himself says that the purpose of the legends is "to give accent to certain values in each scene. Each scene contains a particular point (or several) which is structurally the most important. . . . The legend or image upon the screen will strengthen the effect of what is merely allusion in the writing and allow the primary point to be made more simply and lightly than if the entire responsibility were on the spoken lines." Williams chose to omit the screen device from his final acting version, and some critics have found the legends excessive. For instance, X. J. Kennedy calls the slide projector "a mistake," arguing that "in trying to justify it, Williams underestimates the quality of the play's spoken lines" (Instructor's Guide, *Literature*, 4th ed., Little, Brown).

Going Further

1. Consider ways in which the play is both realistic and non-realistic.

2. Of what importance are dreams to Laura, Amanda, and Tom? To what extent are their dreams illusory? To what extent are they based on reality?

3. What is Jim's role in the play? What does he represent?

4. Who is the protagonist in the play? Amanda? Tom? Laura? Explain and defend your choice, using details and examples from the play.

5. How is the social and historical background of the play's setting important?

The Gap

Eugène Ionesco (b. 1912)

Born to a Rumanian father and a French mother in Rumania, Eugène Ionesco was raised primarily in France and, in fact, did not learn the Rumanian language until he was 13 (his plays are written in French). He studied at the University of Bucharest and became a French teacher while he also wrote poetry and literary criticism, but he was 36 before he began to write drama. He had just undertaken the study of English conversation and became intrigued by the dialogues between characters in his English textbook. He was amused at the conversations between the fictional Mr. and Mrs. Smith, who informed each other of the most mundane facts: The plates were on the table; the food, on the plates; the table, on the floor. From these characters, Ionesco moved to his absurdist vision of the world, where characters who fail to recognize each other's basic qualities and needs spend time explaining perfectly obvious facts. Ionesco's first play *The Bald Soprano* (1949) "established the simple plot, mechanical dehumanized characters, and exaggeratedly absurd language that were to become the marks of his early plays—characteristics that are still by and large identified with his works" (Leonard C. Pronko in *Eugène Ionesco*, Columbia University Press, 1965).

Teaching the Play

Students, as part of the academic world, will readily recognize familiar characteristics in Ionesco's exaggerated stereotypes.

Summary of The Gap

The Friend arrives early in the morning at the home of The Academician and informs The Wife that her husband has failed (we don't know yet at what). After several exchanges, with The Wife expressing extreme distress and The Friend trying to reassure her, The Academician enters, and we learn that what he has failed is the examination to be granted an undergraduate, baccalaureate degree. Since he has many doctoral diplomas hanging on the wall, this seems a strange circumstance. In the course of the play, we discover that, through some error, The Academician never finished the second half of his baccalaureate degree but was somehow allowed to go on and complete more advanced degrees. When confronted with this gap in his record, The Academician offered to take the exam, claiming that this was completely fair. He was unable, however, to succeed. He received a zero in mathematics, Greek, and Latin, and although he received 900 points (which is either a perfect score or less than passing; it is unclear) in composition, we later discover that the answer he has written is nearly incomprehensible. The Academician is furious and tries to contact the university president to have the test declared null and void. The president, however, refuses to speak to The Academician, who is left furiously ripping his diplomas off the wall as The Wife begs him not to do so because "That's all we've got left."

Discussion and Writing Activities

1. Identify the qualities of The Gap *that make it comic. What noncomic features does the play possess? How would you characterize, classify, or otherwise describe the play overall?*

The opening scene leads us to believe that some tragic failure has occurred, so when we find out that the famous Academician has not passed a baccalaureate exam, there is a sense of absurd comedy. It seems that a great deal has been made of nothing. Certainly the ironic view of the unversity is also comic. The president acts like a snobbish child when he tells The Academician, "My mummy won't let me make friends with boys at the bottom of the class." His words emphasize the pettiness of much academic posturing. And of course the idea of a movie star acting as the mathematics examiner or one of the Beatles as the examiner for Greek is ludicrous and pathetically funny. The play is noncomic because it reveals some ugly truths about the world of academe and brings into question both the quality of education received at universities as well as methods of examination. This play certainly qualifies as absurdist drama, but as we watch the broken Academician tearing his diplomas off the wall, it also becomes a tragicomedy.

2. To what extent is The Gap *a play about education and learning? To what extent is it about social or psychological issues?*

The Academician is a man who has been forced to realize that he does not measure up to his own view of himself. Further, he has been forced to recognize that the standards he has always seen as absolute and which he has imposed on others are quite possibly unfair and unrealistic. Although the structure used to convey this painful enlightening concerns the academic world, similar crises occur in the lives of many people who have devoted their entire careers to endeavors they come to recognize in mid-life as absurd. On the other hand, many specific criticisms are made of the academic world. Its dependence on degrees, on examinations, on honors won or lost to judge the worth of a person as well as the worth of his or her ideas comes in for a well-deserved satiric attack.

3. What actually is the "gap," and why is it so important to The Academician? To the educational bureaucracy?

The "gap" refers to The Academician's lack of the second half of his baccalaureate degree. Since both he and the educational bureaucracy have viewed the ordered progression from one class to the next, from one diploma and degree to the next, as essential, the gap represents a challenge. How could someone possibly have won advanced degrees and even the Nobel Prize (three times!) without having passed through the gauntlet that The Academician has believed—and the educational bureaucracy has insisted upon—as necessary? The Academician foolishly feels the need to prove himself rather than simply pointing out the achievements he has made, and he discovers to his sorrow that he cannot, in fact, pass the test that he has for years insisted others pass in order to get their credentials to enter the next phase of their lives.

4. What do the stage setting and costumes contribute to the spirit and effect of the play?

The comfortable upper middle-class life-style reflected by the furniture suggests the complacency and smugness with which The Academician regards his life. The walls of his home are covered with various diplomas, especially honorary degrees that he has clearly won because of his venerated position in the academic world. His display of honors shows that The Academician bases his sense of self-worth on these pieces of paper, and most audiences will agree that he is excessively proud of his awards. Most people, after all, do not decorate their living rooms with framed copies of their degrees. The Academician's pompous attire (full-dress uniform covered with decorations and with a sword at his side) underlines his hunger for the outward show of honors collected. Both setting and costumes establish a spirit of comic exaggeration.

5. How should the roles of The Wife and The Friend be acted? Why don't any of the characters have traditional names?

The characters lack traditional names because they represent types rather than individuals. The Wife is the typical ambitious woman who gets her identity from her husbànd rather than from her own accomplishments. The Friend is the standard "bearer of bad tidings" who seems to take a certain pleasure in undermining each honor The Academician holds. The Academician himself, of course, is a stereotype of the unfeeling, unthinking professor who prides himself on past accomplishments, shows little mercy toward his students, and demands "standards"—except when they are suddenly applied to him.

6. *What kind of audience do you think would be most receptive to a staging of this play? Who might be least receptive?*

People who are suspicious of authority figures in general and academics in particular will love this play. An audience of students about to face exams should find it hilarious. How would an audience of professors receive the play? In general, academicians tend to find this play quite funny, perhaps because few people see themselves in the professor's shoes. No one wants to admit he or she is a fraud, basing a career on foolish standards. On the other hand, humorless teachers and professors who believe they have to defend their territory at all costs may find the portrait cuts too close to home to be funny.

Going Further

1. *At first the play seems to be realistic or at least plausible. At what point does it become clear that the action, setting, and characters belong to an absurd world that can be considered believable only in an exaggerated and symbolic sense?*

2. *The Wife accuses The Academician of taking the exam only because he wants to gain more honors. Do you agree? What other possible motives might he have? Explain your answer.*

3. *How does the attitude of The Academician toward the academic process change as the play progresses? How can you account for this change?*

4. *How valid do you find Ionesco's criticisms of the academic world? Do his criticisms apply to high schools as well as to universities and colleges? Explain your answer.*

5. *Write a scene showing* The Academician *back in a classroom, teaching, after he has gone through the experience of failing his baccalaureate examination.*

A View from the Bridge

Arthur Miller (b. 1915)

The son of an Austrian immigrant who worked as a clothing manufacturer, Arthur Miller grew up in Brooklyn, New York, where he watched developments and changes that became part of the setting of both *Death of a Salesman* (perhaps his best-known play) and *A View from the Bridge.* When Miller graduated from high school, he was unable to go to college because, as he put it, "nobody in the house was in possession of the fare" (from *The Harper American Literature,* Vol. 2, Harper & Row, 1987). Determined to earn the money for an education, he worked for more than two years in an automobile-parts warehouse, where his experiences with the motivations, sorrows, hopes, and commitments of working men greatly contributed to the storehouse that he drew upon for several of his plays, including *A View from the Bridge.*

When he had saved enough money, Miller left his job and attended the University of Michigan, where he began to write drama. He won two awards while still in college and in his graduation year, 1938, also won the Theater Guild National Award.

After working at various jobs, among them driving a truck and waiting on tables, Miller began to publish successfully, including a novel called *Focus,* which addresses anti-Semitism. Always committed to social justice, Miller adapted Ibsen's *An Enemy of the People* in 1950 and later wrote two plays, *The Crucible* and *After the Fall,* which relate to public hysteria and persecution of the innocent. Although *The Crucible* cannot be read as an exact allegory, certainly Miller's ordeals with the House Committee on Un-

American Activities hearings are reflected in *After the Fall. Incident at Vichy,* produced in 1964, deals with Nazi crimes before World War II, continuing Miller's concern with social injustice.

Teaching the Play

Arthur Miller is most appreciated for his plays focusing on family dramas, intertwining the themes of relationships and the world of work. Both *All My Sons* and *Death of a Salesman* show a father in conflict with his two sons, and in both plays the father's work (and the way he views his work) is of primary importance. *A View from the Bridge,* written several years after those two plays, once again deals with the conflict between the older and younger generations.

Summary of A View from the Bridge

Alfieri, a lawyer, serves as a narrator and commentator as well as taking part in this drama. He opens the play by describing the working-class people who are his clients and by describing in free verse the "view from the bridge," the scene he sees and the speculations he makes as he gazes out from his office looking over Red Hook, the "slum that faces the bay,/Seaward from Brooklyn Bridge." His chant suggests that the emotions felt by even apparently ordinary people go back to primal, ancestral origins and relate them to their roots in ancient Rome.

Eddie, his wife, Beatrice, and their seventeen-year-old niece, Catherine (the daughter of Beatrice's sister), prepare for the arrival of Beatrice's cousins, illegal immigrants who will be staying with them. Eddie is kind about the coming arrivals, but keeps after Catherine to take off the high-heeled shoes that he thinks make her look too old and seductive. This opening scene shows Eddie as a good family man, concerned about his wife and perhaps a bit overly concerned with his niece. Conversation also indicates the precarious status of illegal immigrants but shows the general acceptance of such workers in the neighborhood and the disdain accorded anyone who would turn such men over to the authorities.

When Rodolpho, the unmarried cousin, and Marco, the married cousin, arrive, the family seems to get along at first. Catherine, however, is particularly taken with the blond Rodolpho, which makes Eddie very nervous. Alfieri is spotlighted from time to time, commenting on the seemingly minor events that will build to a tragic climax. Catherine and Rodolpho begin to go to the movies together and are clearly taken with each other. Eddie behaves in a very overprotective manner and argues with Beatrice about how much freedom the young woman should have. After a conversation with several of his friends who hint that Rodolpho is "funny" in a strange way, Eddie becomes even more upset and tries to convince Catherine that Rodolpho is only courting her because he wants to marry an American to gain legal status. Eddie goes to Alfieri to try to stop Rodolpho from pursuing Catherine, hinting that the young man is a homosexual and offering such evidence as his high singing voice and his ability to sew. Alfieri urges Eddie to forget the idea and gently points out that Eddie may be too deeply involved emotionally with Catherine. Tension increases and one night Eddie, under the guise of teaching Rodolpho to box, punches the young man. Marco counters by demonstrating his strength to Eddie in a chair-lifting contest that Marco wins.

Near Christmastime, Eddie returns from work early one evening, a little drunk, and finds Catherine and Rodolpho alone in the apartment. Earlier action suggests that Catherine and Rodolpho have just made love, and Eddie gets furious. In his anger he kisses Catherine on the lips and in a fury pins Rodolpho down and kisses him, too. Once again, Eddie goes to Alfieri, trying to prove that Rodolpho should not be allowed to marry Catherine because he is a homosexual. And once again, Alfieri tells him the law would not stand on his side.

Desperate, Eddie calls the immigration authorities and anonymously reports his wife's cousins. When he returns to his apartment, the cousins have moved out and into an upstairs apartment with a neighbor who, Eddie now realizes, is harboring two "submarines" (illegal aliens) herself. He panics when he understands what will happen; not only will Rodolpho and Marco be deported, the neighbor's illegal relatives will also be deported. Eddie will be an outcast in the neighborhood. His actions cannot be wished away, however. Two immigration agents arrive and arrest the cousins as well as the other illegal residents. As they are taken away,

Marco spits on Eddie and accuses him in front of the assembled neighbors who are watching the events.

Alfieri goes to the jail to bail the brothers out and tries unsuccessfully to make Marco promise he will not seek revenge. Rodolpho and Catherine intend to get married, and Catherine goes to beg Beatrice to attend the ceremony. Eddie forbids his wife to leave, and during the quarrel Rodolpho enters the apartment with the news that Marco is coming to get revenge. Eddie refuses to run, believing he has done nothing wrong, and is confused about how everything has gone awry. When Beatrice refers to Rodolpho as Catherine's husband, Eddie cries out in anguish that he is her lover, and he kisses her passionately. Beatrice tries to convince Eddie to leave, but she is too late. Marco arrives, and he and Eddie fight each other with a knife. Eddie is killed, piteously asking, "Catherine—why—?" and clearly failing to understand what has happened.

Alfieri closes with a narration that picks up the timeless images of the opening chant.

Discussion and Writing Topics

1. What is Alfieri's role in the play? To what extent can he be compared to the choragos in a Greek tragedy?

In a Greek play, the choragos functions as the leader of the chorus, voicing the conscience of the community. Unlike the chorus, the choragos interacts with the other characters in the play, provoking the main character to examine issues and implications of actions. Alfieri definitely fits this definition. He appears at significant points in the drama to explain what is happening and to predict the outcome of the events that are set in motion. As the lawyer of this blue-collar community, he speaks both with authority and with understanding of his constituents' values. Certainly the verse format of his opening and closing speeches suggests the rhythm of Greek dramatists like Sophocles. In addition, Alfieri is the one character who seems to understand clearly what is going on inside Eddie's heart and head and who tries to get Eddie to understand himself. He sees the danger of Eddie's deep, probably incestuous, feelings for his niece but cannot convince his distraught client to back away from the disaster that so clearly lies ahead.

2. *To what extent is Miller's play a realistic drama, presenting a slice of life in ethnic New York? Do you see any evidence that* A View from the Bridge *is more a classic tragedy than a realistic drama?*

Although the Brooklyn dialect and the situation (illegal immigrants seeking refuge) are modern and realistic, there are many aspects of the play that suggest classic tragedy. As discussed in question 1 (above), Alfieri serves as the choragos who comments on and analyzes the action of the main character. Eddie may not qualify as a person of high estate, but in many ways he seems like a tragic hero. He is basically a decent, honorable man, as Alfieri assures us. He works hard, respects his wife, and cares for his children. As the drama progresses, however, it becomes clear that he also has a tragic flaw—his passionate obsession with Catherine. He is unable either to recognize or to control this obsession, and it leads him inexorably to his death in the final scene. In addition to these larger aspects, there are smaller parts of the play that suggest the ancient roots of this story. For instance, when Alfieri sees what is happening, he goes to consult a wise old woman who sees the inevitable and simply advises him to pray for Eddie. She might represent the oracle of a Greek tragedy who can see the future and yet gives only enigmatic advice when asked.

3. *Explain why Eddie is upset with Catherine and Rodolpho. How much of what he is feeling does his wife, Beatrice, understand? How much does Alfieri understand?*

Beatrice understands very little of what is happening to her husband, whereas Alfieri sees the relationships clearly and willingly risks Eddie's anger by warning him about the dangers of remaining too close to Catherine. Students may not fully recognize Eddie's romantic inclinations toward Catherine because they may be willing to buy Eddie's rationalizations about Rodolpho. Because Rodolpho does not conform to Eddie's stereotyped ideas of manhood, Eddie convinces himself that his wife's cousin is homosexual ("not right") and therefore must be prevented from marrying Catherine. The situation in reality is that Eddie himself loves Catherine. The

A View from the Bridge

kiss he gives her after he discovers her alone with Rodolpho as well as the embrace at the end of the play show the depth of his feelings. He believes that he, not Rodolpho, should be Catherine's lover. Beatrice sees the situation through the eyes of a loving wife and aunt. She recognizes that Eddie is overprotective but is completely shocked and surprised by the revelations at the end of the play. Alfieri, as discussed in question 1 (above), sees what is happening and tells Eddie, going so far as to compare his feelings to the incestuous responses a father may have for his daughter. Neither Beatrice's innocence nor Alfieri's knowledge can help Eddie, who cannot let go of his deep attachment to Catherine.

4. *To what extent do Eddie's accusations against Rodolpho seem justified?*

Eddie accuses Rodolpho of using Catherine, but the young man seems to be guilty only of a flamboyant personality and mannerisms that annoy Eddie. For example, Eddie claims that Rodolpho wants to marry Catherine only so he can stay in the United States, yet the confrontation between Catherine and Rodolpho over this issue indicates the young man's sincerity. He refuses to say that he will return to his Italian village (where all indications are that economic conditions are desperate) and instead points out to Catherine that he would be a fool to take on the responsibility of a wife if he did not really love her. Students may differ on their views as to whether or not Rodolpho is, in fact, homosexual. Certainly Eddie's bases for judgment are almost laughably superficial. Rodolpho is blond, can sing high notes, and can sew. The scene between Rodolpho and Catherine alone is almost certainly meant by Miller to put to rest the suspicions of Rodolpho's sexuality that Eddie has raised. Though we know today that sexual preferences are not necessarily clear-cut, at the time the play was written Catherine and Rodolpho's disappearance into the bedroom would have been proof of Rodolpho's heterosexuality.

5. *Describe your reaction to the play, your emotional response to the characters, their situations, and their actions. Which characters do you consider to be the most and the least sympathetic, and why?*

To use this question for an in-class exercise, ask students to rank the following characters from 1 to 5 according to how much sympathy they have for each: Eddie, Catherine, Beatrice, Marco, and Rodolpho (a rating of 1 equals the greatest sympathy; 5, the least). Then ask them to meet in groups, compare decisions, and try to reach a consensus. Each person, then, will try to convince the others to agree to his or her hierarchy. Set a time limit (15 to 20 minutes works well), and then ask one student from each group to report the group's progress to the class. Not only should the listing be reported but also the reasons for the group's decisions.

6. *Look carefully at the scene in which Eddie gives Rodolpho a boxing lesson. How could the actor who portrays Eddie show what is going on inside his character during this scene? How could each of the onlookers convey his or her reactions?*

Eddie is very angry during this scene and wants to "teach Rodolpho a lesson" about life rather than about boxing. The actor who plays Eddie should convey tension and barely controlled fury as he toys with Rodolpho. The onlookers register their discomfort. Perhaps the women move slightly toward the two boxers as if to intervene. Marco becomes more and more aware of what is happening and moves to show his own tension and growing anger at Eddie's merciless taunting and abuse of his brother.

7. *Part of the play's intensity stems from its being performed in close quarters, in a cramped physical space. Select a unit of action and explain how you would stage it, especially how you would group and move the characters.*

Scenes that work well for this exercise include these: the first meeting of Eddie, Beatrice, and Catherine with Marco and Rodolpho; the boxing lesson scene; the encounter between Eddie, Catherine, and Rodolpho when Eddie finds the pair alone in the apartment.

Going Further

1. *Miller goes to some trouble to suggest that Eddie can't stop himself from feeling as he does or from acting on his feelings. To what extent is he responsible for his actions and for their consequences?*

2. *Identify the discrepancy between Eddie's view of himself and the views of him taken by other characters, including Catherine, Marco, and Alfieri.*

3. *Describe Eddie's relationship with his wife, Beatrice, and with his niece, Catherine.*

4. *What function is served by Mr. and Mrs. Lipari and their two "submarines"? What do they contribute to the conflict and its resolution?*

5. *Arthur Miller has written that "the common man is as apt a subject for tragedy as kings" and that "the tragic feeling is evoked in us when we are in the presence of a character who is ready to lay down his life to secure his dignity." To what extent do these observations apply to Eddie Carbone?*

A Raisin in the Sun

Lorraine Hansberry (1930–1965)

As the youngest of four children born into a middle-class black family on Chicago's South Side in 1930, Lorraine Hansberry spent the early years of her childhood relatively isolated from racial prejudice. This all changed, however, when she was 8 years old and her father, Carl Augustus Hansberry, a prominent Chicago banker and real estate broker, deliberately decided to move his family into one of Chicago's restricted white neighborhoods. The move ultimately resulted in a civil rights case that went all the way to the United States Supreme Court, with Hansberry emerging as the victor. But the fight had not been an easy one, and the "crackers" referred to in *A Raisin in the Sun* expressed their hatred toward the family with both verbal and physical violence. In a letter written less than one year before her death, Lorraine Hansberry still vividly recalled being spat at and cursed at daily as she walked to school, while at home her mother actually kept a loaded gun to protect her four children. It is this concept of courage in the face of injustice that permeates the works of Hansberry.

In high school, Hansberry found her love for theater, and she expressed her ambition to become a journalist in her high school yearbook. She attended the University of Wisconsin, where she was particularly fascinated with the Irish playwright Sean O'Casey, but her stay at the university was short-lived. Hansberry felt the need to practice her art, and shortly after attending a speech by Frank Lloyd Wright in which he attacked the nature of education, she set out for New York City to begin her career as a writer.

Honors came to the playwright at an early age. On March 11, 1959, at the Ethel Barrymore Theatre, Hansberry's *A Raisin in the Sun* had its New York debut. Within two months, up against such dramatists as Eugene O'Neill, Tennessee Williams, and Archibald MacLeish, Lorraine Hansberry became the fifth woman, the only black, and the youngest American playwright to win the New York Drama Circle Critics Award for best play of the year. One month later, in June 1959, she was named most promising playwright by *Variety*. *A Raisin in the Sun* ran for 530 performances, and soon after the termination of the stage production, a film version starring Sidney Poitier and Claudia McNeil was released by Columbia Pictures. Ironically, Hansberry's second play, *The Sign in Sidney Brustein's Window,* which ran on Broadway for 101 performances, closed on January 12, 1965, the day of Hansberry's untimely death from cancer at age 34. Hansberry's love of all cultures and her ability to relate to the struggles of humanity have won her a place among the great American playwrights of the twentieth century.

Teaching the Play

This play is set in Chicago's South Side in the early 1950s. Students need to know that the Civil Rights Movement of the 1960s had not yet taken place and that abortions, illegal in this country, were performed without the services of legitimate doctors and hospitals.

Summary of A Raisin in the Sun

Act I, Scene I   As the play opens, we are introduced to Ruth

Younger, who no longer listens to the risk-taking schemes of her husband, Walter. Instead, she attempts to nurture the physical rather than the more demanding emotional side of her husband. Their son, Travis, highlights their differences when Walter brashly gives him the money which practical Ruth has just denied him. The dominance of Walter's mother also emerges in this early scene as she attempts to take over Ruth's nurturing role of Travis. In addition, Walter demonstrates his jealousy of his sister Beneatha and his resentment of her determination to rise above their stagnant existence. Mama questions Beneatha but still allows her "to flit so from one thing to another" while Walter is "choking to death" in his present situation. Throughout this scene there is much talk about a check—from the life insurance of Mama's late husband—that is due in the mail.

Act I, Scene II   Mama is reluctant to receive callers while in the midst of her Saturday cleaning, but Joseph Asagai, a Nigerian whom Beneatha has met at college, invades not only the apartment but also Beneatha's concept of self. Asagai awakens in Beneatha her sense of her African roots. As traditional as Mama may appear on many issues, she does alter her stereotyped image of African blacks and reaches out to attempt to understand Asagai's culture.

When the life insurance check finally arrives, Mama is saddened by Walter's obsession with the money, available only because of his father's death. All Walter wants is Mama's support for his dream of owning a liquor store. During the ensuing argument over spending the money, Mama tells Walter that Ruth is pregnant and considering an abortion. This news only serves to sink Walter further into his sense of entrapment, and he refuses to tell Ruth to keep the baby. Mama and Walter, both disgusted, leave separately.

Act II, Scene I   Act II opens with Beneatha dressed in the Nigerian robes Asagai has given to her. A drunken Walter joins in as she attempts to discover her roots in native dance. George Murchison, a "successful" young black friend of Beneatha's, comes to pick her up for a date, and Walter criticizes his affected "college boy" ways. George symbolizes the assimilationist who has deserted his native roots in favor of the business and educational status of white America.

Mama returns home to announce that she has made a down payment on a house in Clybourne Park, a white neighborhood where she was able to get more house for her money. Walter accuses her of butchering his dreams and again storms out.

Act II, Scene II Home from another date, a few weeks later, Beneatha realizes that she has little in common with George, and she warmly thanks Mama for understanding. Walter's boss calls, and Walter confesses that he hasn't been to work for three days and that "don't nothing matter worth a damn." His extreme disillusion makes Mama realize that she has not allowed him to be a man, and she gives him the remaining $6,500 of the insurance money—$3,000 to be put into an account for Beneatha's education and the other $3,500 to be spent as he chooses. Alone with Travis, Walter starts thinking like a millionaire. It becomes obvious that Walter will not be able to handle the financial responsibility Mama has given him.

Act II, Scene III The family is happily packing when Mr. Lindner of the Clybourne Park "Welcoming Committee" arrives. After his references to the dreams of the people in Clybourne Park, he asks the Youngers to abandon their dreams of advancement by selling their new house back to him. The Youngers show him the door. Mama returns home, and, after telling her about Mr. Lindner's visit, the family gives her gifts of gardening tools and a gardening hat to use at the new house.

The gaiety of the gift-giving scene disappears as Bobo, Walter's business partner, arrives and explains that their investments (including the college fund) have been stolen. Walter reacts strongly to the loss of the money, which was made of his "father's flesh."

Act III Beneatha tells Asagai of her shattered plans. He does not, however, allow her to accept defeat passively but offers her the opportunity and challenge to go with him to Africa. Mama, exhausted from the trials, almost gives up on the idea of moving, but Ruth makes an impassioned plea for the move. Walter returns home to inform the family that they are going to sell out to Lindner, but during the actual meeting proves in front of his family that he is a proud man who will fight for his family's rights. The play ends on a restrained optimistic note as the moving men load the truck, and Mama picks up her "raggedy" plant and heads out for Clybourne Park.

Discussion and Writing Topics

1. *Describe the relationship of Mama (Lena) with her daughter, Beneatha, and with her son, Walter. What expectations does she have for the future of each? Why?*

Mama is both the matriarch of the family and the strongest character of the drama. A woman who has endured much and has survived, she has nonetheless neglected to see how dominant a personality she has become. Beneatha's views sharply contrast with many of her mother's traditional beliefs, and these differences create a strained relationship between the old and the new. For example, like her mother, Beneatha is a fighter, but unlike Mama, Beneatha sees no need for the role of God in her struggle for survival. Both women agree, however, about Beneatha's dream of becoming a doctor, with Mama willing to sacrifice a share of the inheritance for the fulfillment of Beneatha's goal.

Mama cannot accept Walter's dream as easily as she can Beneatha's. With her Christian beliefs, Mama doesn't want it on her "ledger" that she gave money to set up a liquor store. Mama fails to realize that she has become such a dominant force in the family that she has never allowed Walter to become what she most desires him to be—a man. Walter can only become a man when Mama gives him enough space to exercise his manhood.

2. *Identify two explanations for the primary conflicts of the play. What precipitates the various arguments and battles the characters wage with one another?*

Students will quickly realize that life in the Younger family is a far cry from the Brady Bunch, but not so distant a cry, perhaps, from their own families, where members, although often to a much lesser degree, vie for their own dreams without concern for the family unit. In addition, Walter's conflict with everyone must be seen in the light of his race, for his blackness intensifies his struggle. Walter is an angry young man who only asks for the equality that is due him as a man. He questions why he must be a chauffeur and why he must accept the fact that his wife won't have pearls to wear around her neck. He vents his anger on Beneatha, who appears to have beaten the system of prejudice because she will be a doctor; on Ruth, whose "small mind" ties him down to a secure but unfulfilling job; and on Mama, whom he sees as too traditional in her concept of a "proper" business.

3. *Explain the roles of Joseph Asagai and George Murchison. What dramatic role does each assume? Does either have any thematic significance? Explain your answer.*

George represents the black man who wants to deny his heritage, as suggested by his hostile response to Beneatha's interest in African culture. Students may discuss the tradition of ethnic heritage, asking whether the melting pot of America can and should allow for the return of diverse backgrounds within the American dream. George Murchison attempts to wipe out his roots in favor of white educational and business values. His negation of his heritage serves to push Beneatha dramatically closer to Asagai and her search for self while she still retains her dream of becoming a physician.

Beneatha prepares both the reader and Mama for the function of Joseph Asagai as the symbol of black heritage in her wonderful speech on the stereotyped African black. George and Asagai represent two of the forces operating on and within the family as they try to fulfill their dreams. The resolution of the drama suggests that blacks must find individual solutions, acting according to their own life goals and not according to standards set by either the white American or black African culture.

4. *Did you find this play engaging or interesting? Why or why not? What makes it especially an urban play? A "minority" play? In what ways does it transcend these categories?*

In Hansberry's own words, she wrote "about people who happen to be Negroes, rather than Negro plays." The universality of the play's theme, the characters' search for personal freedom and a better existence, allows the drama to transcend the categorical boundaries of urban or minority plays.

5. *Identify two important stage props and comment on their*

role in the play. Discuss whether either or both may be symbolic and why.

The plant, as Mama notes, "expresses me." Although it is a "raggedy-looking old" thing, she returns for it at the end of the play, recognizing that after having been kept alive for all these years in the cramped apartment, it will now have a chance to grow and thrive in a new environment. The plant's survival reflects the survival of the Younger family. The single window in the apartment also functions symbolically, suggesting the lack of natural sunshine and the corresponding darkness of the Youngers' life within that apartment.

6. *Try to find the Langston Hughes poem "Dream Deferred," from which Hansberry borrowed the title for this play. How is the play a comment on the poem?*

"Dream Deferred" is a widely anthologized poem (for example, it appears in *Reading Poetry,* Random House, 1989) in which Hughes suggests several possible outcomes when a person's dream is repeatedly frustrated. Students should be able to see how the tensions in the Younger family serve to illustrate Hughes's poem.

7. *Some readers consider this play a modern American classic. What do you think may have led them to such an assessment?*

Hansberry addresses themes common to American drama: family struggle and the search for identity. For example, Walter, who experiences a sense of isolation and an erosion of family, can be compared to the major characters in plays by Tennessee Williams, Arthur Miller, and (more recently) Sam Shepard.

8. *Select a scene you find compelling, and describe how you would stage it. Consider especially the close quarters that the three generations must share.*

Possible scenes include: Beneatha's expression of atheism (Act I, Scene I); Asagai presenting the robes and records to Beneatha (Act I, Scene II); Walter's "will somebody please listen to me" scene (Act I, Scene II); Walter's confronting George Murchison (Act II, Scene I); and Mama and Ruth discussing Walter's coming into his manhood (Act III).

Going Further

1. *Identify and discuss a major theme of the play. Support your ideas by referring to specific events and speeches.*

2. *Are you satisfied with the play's ending? Why or why not?*

3. *How do you envision the future of the family, particularly of Ruth, Walter, and Beneatha?*

4. *Evaluate the character of Mr. Lindner. Is he merely a plot device? Is he a stereotype, or do you find him believable? Explain your answer.*

5. *A Raisin in the Sun was first produced in 1959. Do you find the attitudes, actions, and conflicts in the play outdated, or are they still relevant today? Explain your answer.*

True West

Sam Shepard (b. 1943)

Sam Shepard (Samuel Shepard Rogers) was born while his father was serving in the army as a bombardier in Europe. When his father was wounded and returned to the States, the family began a series of moves from one army base to another that lasted until 1955. The family finally settled in California in 1955, and young Sam became fascinated with films, which provided him with an imaginative escape from his everyday life. In *Motel Chronicles* (City Lights, 1982), a collection of autobiographical essays, Shepard sums up his love affair with the movies, writing, "I keep praying for a double bill of *Bad Day at Black Rock* and *Vera Cruz*." In addition to films, music deeply affected Shepard during his teenage years. His father played in a Dixieland combo, and he developed an affinity for jazz. In 1963, at age 19, Shepard left his family and moved alone to New York City, where he worked as a waiter at a popular jazz club and became interested in theater. He listened to some of the best American jazz musicians, and their improvisations served as models for the structure of several of his early plays. Shepard's first play, *Cowboys,* was produced in 1964 and earned the fledgling playwright rave reviews from the prestigious newspaper *The Village Voice.* From that time on, not a year went by that Shepard didn't write drama, screenplays, stories, essays, or poetry. He has published prolifically and continues to write, act in, and direct films and plays. Shepard has won several Obie awards for distinguished plays; in 1979, he was awarded the Pulitzer Prize for *Buried Child.*

Teaching the Play

In this play, Shepard examines and challenges typically American (particularly Western American) assumptions, actions, and beliefs. As an introduction to the play, you can ask students to list characters and behavior patterns that they consider typical of the "Old West" and of the "Hollywood West" of today. As they read the play, ask them to note which of these conventions Shepard uses and how he uses them.

Summary of True West

Act I   The play takes place entirely in the kitchen of a Southern California home. Austin, a writer, is staying in the house, which belongs to his mother, who has taken a vacation trip to Alaska. He dresses in a casual but stylish manner and looks neat, clean, and well put-together. Lee, Austin's brother, has apparently returned to visit his mother and instead finds his brother in residence. In contrast to the rather slight and precisely dressed Austin, Lee is bulky and wears old, worn, soiled clothing that makes him look like a bum. Austin speaks standard, bland, "correct" English; Lee's colorful speech is peppered with "Old West" colloquialisms, grammatical errors, and casual obscenity.

The two brothers are clearly opposites and immediately get into an argument about Austin's Ivy League background and his middle-class standards. Lee tries to take over the house, but Austin firmly refuses. Not to be put off, Lee insists that Austin loan him his car, even though Austin knows his brother will use it as the means to steal goods from the neighbors. Austin, who is trying to concentrate on his writing, finally agrees (at least partly because he expects a visit from Saul Kimmer, who has expressed interest in the script Austin is researching). Later, Lee fulfills Austin's worst fears when he breaks in on his brother's discussion with Kimmer. Lee carries a television (obviously stolen) but manages to fast-talk Kimmer into considering an idea he has for a "true-to-life Western." Austin, upset and filled with disbelief, agrees to type an outline as Lee dictates his story.

Act II Lee returns from playing golf with Kimmer and announces that not only has he maneuvered a contract for himself but he has also convinced Kimmer that Austin ought to do the screenplay for Lee's idea. Austin immediately protests, saying that he only has time for his own project, but Lee gleefully informs his brother that Kimmer has decided to drop Austin's proposal. Austin, who is furious, demands his car keys back and threatens to drive out into the desert. At this point the brother who came from the desert is now a blossoming playwright; the brother who began as a writer expresses his desire to disappear into the desert.

As the play progresses, each brother takes on some of the other's characteristics while still remaining in other ways true to the personality we saw in Act I. Lee sits at the typewriter and tries to write while Austin gets obnoxiously drunk and threatens to terrorize the neighborhood as Lee had done. Lee gets nowhere with his scriptwriting since he no longer has Austin to supply the words he needs, so he, too, gets drunk, then whacks the typewriter with a golf club and destroys the kitchen. Austin has staggered back into the kitchen with an armload of toasters which he has clearly stolen from the neighbors, sets up the toasters, and now proceeds to make toast in all of them at once. Austin pleads with Lee to take him back to the desert, but Lee first refuses, then knocks the toast from Austin's hands and makes his brother grovel in front of him by picking it up. Lee finally agrees to take Austin to the desert, but Austin must once again serve as his secretary.

As Lee shouts bits of dialogue to the frantic Austin, Mom arrives at the door and looks in stunned horror at her kitchen. The two brothers stand before her like the ill-behaved children they are and regard her silently. Austin finally tells her about his plan to live with Lee, but Lee tries to escape (taking his mother's china with him). The brothers scuffle, Austin chokes Lee with a telephone cord, and, as Lee's body falls to the floor, Mom announces her intention to stay at a motel and walks out. Austin fears he has killed his brother and stands back from him, but once more the sly Lee surprises Austin. Lee jumps to his feet and the play ends with the conflict unresolved and the two brothers facing off against each other in their mother's wrecked kitchen.

Discussion and Writing Topics

1. In his prefatory stage directions, Shepard identifies the "characters' situation" as the most important aspect of the play. How would you describe their situation, and how does Shepard dramatize it?

The situation in this play is that two brothers are forced to face not only their differences with each other but also the conflicts within themselves. Austin claims to value his middle-class life-style and his ambitions as an intellectual and a writer. Lee asserts that the suburban California life has lost all touch with the essence of the Old West. He argues that his mother's house and neighborhood represent a falseness and phoniness he holds in disdain. While each brother claims to prefer his own way of living and criticizes the other, we soon see Lee sweet-talking himself into a contract for a screenplay. Austin, distraught and disappointed about losing a similar contract, undergoes a similar role reversal. He begins to talk with a heavy Western drawl, gets roaring drunk, and even sets out on a round of petty thievery. Shepard uses the external conflicts of the brothers to reflect their internal conflicts. Each enjoys certain parts of his own life but feels also the pull of the other's life.

2. Although True West *is a serious play, it also possesses moments of humor. Point out two comic scenes, and explain the source of the humor.*

There are many darkly humorous scenes in *True West*. Certainly one occurs at the beginning of Act II when Lee returns from his meeting with Kimmer and describes their highly improbable golf game. Lee here becomes the prototypical American confidence man. He claims to have set Kimmer up so that he could easily manipulate him into granting him a contract. Lee casually reports the details of the game as Austin becomes more and more incredulous. Austin plays the straight man to Lee's comedian. As the reports of the game and Kimmer's reactions become increasingly extreme, Austin continues to congratulate his brother. But when Lee breaks the news that Austin's project will be dropped, Austin realizes that both he and Kimmer have been bamboozled by the clever Lee.

Another outstandingly humorous scene depends on visual slapstick rather than ironic reversal for its comic effect. When Austin returns with the stolen toasters, sets them up all in a row, and begins to make toast in all of them at the same time, the image is ludicrous, extreme, and underlines the absurdity of the sudden reversal in the two brothers' fortunes. As the scene progresses and Lee uses the toast to make Austin grovel, we see Shepard's talent for turning even broad, physical humor into a grim statement.

3. Shepard has admired Sophocles' dialogue, describing it as "simple rawboned language" that is "terse, cut to the bone and pointed to the heart." Cite examples of Shepard's own dialogue in True West *that either meet or fail to meet this stylistic goal. Explain how and why it does.*

One particularly successful bit of dialogue comes near the end of Scene VIII. The operator has just hung up on Lee while he was trying to convince her to give him the phone numbers of ten women who have his girlfriend's name. Austin urges Lee to have some toast and there ensues a rapid-fire exchange of dialogue as the two brothers reveal their deep differences. Austin claims that he loves beginnings and pleads with Lee to take him to the desert. Lee returns that he's always "been kinda' partial to endings myself." Each line, even when it seems to be a non sequitur mixing desert living skills with making toast, contributes to the sense of extremes and polar opposites represented both by and within the two men.

4. Look carefully at Shepard's set description and directions for staging. What impression of the world of the play do they create?

What kind of environment does the playwright depict, and what is his attitude toward it?

The comfortable, sunny kitchen in which the play takes place suggests a typical suburban home, filled with mechanical and electrical gadgets to make life easy. The hanging plants show the attempt to cultivate nature and keep it under control. By the end of the play, the kitchen lies in ruins, indicating the chaos Shepard sees behind the thin veneer of civilization symbolized by toasters, telephones, and Boston ferns.

5. *Identify the major sounds of the play and comment on their significance.*

Shepard notes in his opening directions that the yapping of the coyotes and the chirping of the crickets are the play's major sound devices. As the play picks up pace and the tensions rise, the coyotes' barking becomes increasingly frenzied. The coyotes represent the wild, the Old West, and its claim on both brothers. Crickets, on the other hand, commonly sing near houses, and a cricket on the hearth is traditionally considered a sign of domestic good fortune. The quiet singing of the crickets is drowned out by the coyotes' calls.

6. *What is typically American about this play? What is typically Western? Consider its language, setting, and implied values.*

Students may want to consider the meaning of the phrase "true west." Does the title imply the Old West, as represented by the twang and slang of Lee as well as by his rough-and-ready way of life? Or does it refer to Hollywood glamour, comfortable suburban homes, and "power" golf games with film producers, as represented by Austin, with his refined, educated speech and his high-powered goals and ambitions?

7. *Select a scene and explain how you would stage it. Shepard offers many details to work with—lighting, sound effects, props, and the similarities and differences between the brothers.*

Possible scenes include: the opening meeting between Lee and Austin (Scene I); the meeting between Saul, Austin, and Lee (Scene III); the confrontation when Lee tells Austin that Saul is dropping

Austin's idea (Scene V); the beginning of Scene VIII, when Lee smashes the typewriter and Austin sets up the "borrowed" toasters.

Going Further

1. *How does Shepard characterize Lee and Austin? How do they differ? In what ways are they alike? What keeps them together?*

2. *Write a scene set five years from the time of the play. How do you envision the future of Lee, Austin, and Mom?*

3. *Discuss the plot of the play, focusing particularly on the brothers' reversal of roles. Do its incidents follow convincingly from one another? Why or why not?*

4. *What is Mom's role in the play? What is gained or lost with her arrival in the final scene?*

5. *Why do you think Shepard only refers to the father without making him an actual physical presence? Compare the "Old Man" to the also-absent father in* The Glass Menagerie.

BIOGRAPHIES OF THE
PLAYWRIGHTS

Anton Chekhov (1860–1904), a doctor who practiced medicine very little in his native Russia, is best known as a writer. He is respected for both his short stories and his plays. Chekhov's writing has been admired for its honesty and sensitivity, for its acute reflections of actual experience, and for its uncanny ability to suggest character range and depth without ponderous philosophizing. His plays and many of his stories can be described as comic, but much of his comedy exhibits a gentle and tender solicitousness about his characters. Although his early farce, *A Marriage Proposal* (1887), does not display the depth and subtlety of later plays, such as *The Three Sisters* (1901) or *The Cherry Orchard* (1904), its humor and theatricality are immediately appealing.

Susan Glaspell (1882–1948), American novelist and playwright, was born in Davenport, Iowa. She was one of the cofounders of the Provincetown Players, an influential theatrical company on Cape Cod (Massachusetts) in the early 1900s. With her husband, George Cram Cook, she collaborated on a number of plays, including her one-act satire on Freudian psychoanalysis, *Suppressed Desires,* published in 1916. In the same year Glaspell produced another fine one-act play, *Trifles,* which has continued to be her most frequently performed play.

Isabella Augusta Persse, Lady Gregory (1852–1932) was born in Roxborough, County Galway, Ireland. She began her literary career after her husband (William Henry Gregory, a landowner and member of Parliament) died in 1892. Along with W. B. Yeats and others, she was a founder of the Irish Literary Theatre (1898) and later the Irish National Theatre Society, where she became a director of its famed Abbey Theatre (1904). As patron to Yeats, with her work in the Abbey Theatre where she was a supporter of J. M. Synge, and for her own literary activities, Lady Gregory was well known as one of the leaders of the late nineteenth- and early twentieth-century period known as the Irish Renaissance. She wrote or translated nearly forty plays, as well as collecting and translating old Irish legends and doing studies of Irish folklore. Her plays (both comedies and realistic fantasies, such as *The Image* [1910], *Damer's Gold* [1913], *The Golden Apple* [1916], and *The Dragon* [1920]), are known for vivid dialogue and characterization in their representation of the lives of Irish peasants.

Lorraine Hansberry (1930–1965) was born and raised in Chicago. She studied painting at the Chicago Art Institute and the University of Wisconsin before turning to writing when she moved to New York. *A Raisin in the Sun* (1959), her first Broadway play, was quickly made into a movie starring Sidney Poitier. Although the play reflects Hansberry's deep concern with civil rights, it transcends its largely racial and urban focus. *A Raisin in the Sun*, which dramatizes the powerful attractions of the American dream of success, is primarily concerned with family life in its intimacy, tragedy, and triumph.

Henrik Ibsen (1828–1906), poet and dramatist, was born in Norway. During his early years, Ibsen studied medicine and was a pharmacist's assistant, served as an editor of a weekly magazine, and worked as a stage director. In his thirties he directed the Norwegian National Theater in Oslo. Then he left Norway to live in Italy and Germany, where for nearly thirty years he enjoyed greater artistic freedom to direct and write plays. While abroad, he wrote many of his best-known plays, among them *A Doll's House* (1879), *Ghosts* (1881), *An Enemy of the People* (1882), *The Wild Duck* (1884), and *Hedda Gabler* (1890). Although Ibsen wrote symbolic and poetic dramas, he is renowned for his realistic plays, which combine social criticism with psychological insight and provide illuminating analyses of real human problems. His influence on twentieth-century dramatists has been enormous.

Eugène Ionesco (b. 1912), born in Rumania, has become well known as a playwright and intellectual who writes in French and lives in France. As a major figure of the modernist theater of the absurd, Ionesco is a theatrical ally of Samuel Beckett, creator of the classic absurdist play *Waiting for Godot.* Ionesco's plays, such as *The Bald Soprano* and *The Chairs,* typically emphasize man's alienation and isolation. Often dramatizing problems in communication, they satirize such aspects of modern life as conformity and insensitive bureaucracy. *The Gap* reveals Ionesco's mastery of the short play while demonstrating his penchant for comic exaggeration.

Arthur Miller (b. 1915) was born in Manhattan, grew up in Brooklyn, and was educated at the University of Michigan, where he studied theater and wrote plays. Before he was 30, he had a play produced on Broadway—*The Man Who Had All the Luck.* Within five years, he had written two of his most popular plays: *All My Sons* (1947) and *Death of a Salesman* (1949), which won a Pulitzer Prize. His other notable plays include *The Crucible* (1953), based on the Salem, Massachusetts, witch trials of 1692, and *After the Fall* (1964), which drew on his five-year marriage to Marilyn Monroe. Miller also wrote the screenplay for *The Misfits* (1961), which starred Monroe and Clark Gable. *A View from the Bridge* (1955) is characteristic Miller theater with its realistic dialogue, its characters drawn from the lower middle class, and its conflict that turns on an ethical issue.

Biographies of the Playwrights

Molière (Jean-Baptiste Poquelin, 1622–1673) was born and raised in Paris, where he joined (and eventually became the leader of) a theatrical company that performed both in the city itself and in the provincial environs. His acting troupe eventually came under the sponsorship of King Louis XIV (the Sun King) and became known as The King's Comedians. After Molière's death, which followed almost immediately after he performed in one of his plays (*The Imaginary Invalid*), his company merged with another group, the Comédie Française, which still exists today. Like Shakespeare before him, Molière was a poet and actor as well as a playwright. Molière's genius was limited to comedy. Unlike Shakespeare, who wrote many romantic comedies, Molière's brand of comedy was predominantly satiric. His best-known and most frequently performed plays include *The Miser* (1668), *The Misanthrope* (1666), *Tartuffe* (1667), and *The Bourgeois Gentleman* (1670).

William Shakespeare (1564–1616), poet and dramatist, was born in Stratford-on-Avon, England (hence his nicknames: The Bard of Avon or The Swan of Avon). At age 18, Shakespeare married Anne Hathaway, by whom he had three children (two daughters and a son). Following his marriage, Shakespeare began work as an actor and a playwright, becoming established in London in 1592. Two years later he joined a theatrical company that was called Lord Chamberlain's Men during Queen Elizabeth I's reign. The name was changed in the early 1600s to The King's Men when they came under the sponsorship of King James I. Shakespeare is credited with having written thirty-seven plays. Among them are comedies, such as *Love's Labour's Lost*; tragedies, such as *Hamlet*; history plays, such as *Henry VIII*; and romances, which were his final plays. The last romance, *The Tempest,* was written in 1611. Of all his poetic and dramatic works, Shakespeare's dramatic tragedies stand in highest esteem today. Among these, *Macbeth* is one of the greatest and most enduring. Shakespeare's ability to portray psychological conflict within characters and dramatize their conflicts with action is succinctly represented in this play.

Sam Shepard (b. 1943) was born in Illinois but grew up in Southern California. Perhaps best known as an actor, Shepard has starred in such films as *The Right Stuff, Country, Baby Boom,* and *Crimes of the Heart.* He has disowned many of his more than forty plays as experimental exercises in learning to write for the theater. Among his best-known and critically acclaimed plays are those dealing with family relations and with individual destiny: *Buried Child* (1978), *True West* (1980), and *Fool for Love* (1983). *True West* shows the influence of Greek drama as Shepard strives for spareness and directness. He keeps the sets simple and focuses on only a few characters who engage in emotional revelations and intense personal discoveries. The play also demonstrates Shepard's ear for comic dialogue and his instinct for the comic effects of outrageousness.

Sophocles (496?–406 B.C.), the Greek playwright, lived during the Golden Age of Athens, when its military power and artistic and philosophic achievements were at their zenith. He served as a general with Pericles and was a commissioner of the Athenian empire. However, he is best known and remembered as a dramatist of great tragedies. He wrote over one hundred plays, only seven of which have survived through the centuries. Many of his plays were entered in competition with plays by other Greek tragic dramatists, including Aeschylus and Euripides, whose work he surpassed on at least twenty occasions. Of these three great dramatists, Sophocles is the most widely performed and read today. Unlike Aeschylus, Sophocles focused his plays on human rather than religious concerns. His most famous plays, including *Oedipus Rex,* center on a crisis and portray characters under moral conflict. *Antigonê,* set in Thebes, a city prostrated by war, turns on difficult decisions that both Antigonê and Creon must make.

August Strindberg (1849–1912), Swedish novelist and dramatist, was at various times a schoolteacher, private tutor, librarian, journalist, and actor. Like Henrik Ibsen, Strindberg was an originator of the modern theater. However, where Ibsen's dramas were cast in a predominantly realistic mode, Strindberg experimented more restlessly with other dramatic styles. An intense and passionate man, Strindberg suffered a severe psychological crisis during his forties that influenced his subsequent plays. An innovative playwright, Strindberg sought ways to dramatize the inner worlds of his characters. His greatest plays do this in different ways, from the intense and anguished realism of *The Father* (1887) to the more expressionistic and mysterious *Dance of Death* (1901) and *A Dream Play* (1902). As *The Stronger* (1889) amply demonstrates, Strindberg was a master of the one-act play, compressing into a brief compass the encapsulated inner lives of his characters.

John Millington Synge (1871–1909), like Lady Gregory and William Butler Yeats, was an Irish dramatist who was intensely involved in the Irish Literary Renaissance. With Yeats and Lady Gregory, he served as codirector of the Abbey Theatre in Dublin. At Yeats's suggestion, Synge brought his knowledge and experience of the Irish peasantry, especially from his visits to the Aran Islands, into the language and dramatic situations of his plays. Yeats convinced Synge to abandon writing criticism and to write plays about simple people whose language reflected an intimate contact with earth, sea, and sky. In addition to *Riders to the Sea* (1904), which shows the extent to which Synge took Yeats's advice, Synge is best known for the masterful comedy *The Playboy of the Western World* (1907). His journal of impressions (*The Aran Islands*) provides important information about the life of the island people and a helpful glimpse into the raw material Synge shaped into dramatic art.

Tennessee Williams (1911–1983) was born in Mississippi with the name Thomas Lanier Williams. He grew up mostly in St. Louis, but later he traveled and lived in other areas of the country, especially the South. He used the South as the setting for some of his most famous plays, including *A Streetcar Named Desire* (1947), for which he received a Pulitzer Prize, and *Cat on a Hot Tin Roof* (1955), which also was awarded a Pulitzer

Prize. *The Glass Menagerie* (1945) was Williams's first commercial success and critical success, receiving the award of the New York Drama Critics Circle. One of America's greatest dramatists, Williams is known for searing dramas of family and interpersonal relationships as well as for his complicated women characters, who are both fragile and strong, pathetic and heroic. *The Glass Menagerie* is a loosely autobiographical, though impressionistic, rendition of his family.

William Butler Yeats (1865–1939), Irish poet and playwright, was born in Dublin and grew up in London, Dublin, and Sligo (in western Ireland). In 1898, with the assistance of other playwrights, most notably Lady Gregory, Yeats founded the Irish Literary Theatre, which later became the Irish National Theatre Society and the Abbey Theatre. His dramatic works include *The Countess Cathleen* (1892), *The Land of Heart's Desire* (1894), *Cathleen ni Houlihan* (1902), *Deirdre* (1907), and *The Herne's Egg* (1938). Although most of his plays center on Irish legend and folklore, others reflect the concerns of his time. *Purgatory,* in its scenic starkness and ritualistic action, displays the influence of Japanese Nō theater and of Greek drama, especially Sophoclean tragedy.

JUDITH A. STANFORD teaches literature and writing at Rivier College in Nashua, New Hampshire. She received her B.A. from Colby College, in Waterville, Maine, and her M.A. and Ph.D. from the University of California at Santa Barbara. She is co-author of *The Writing Connection*, a college composition textbook, and is one of the authors of the second edition of *The Art of Reading* (McGraw-Hill Publishing Company). She has consulted extensively and written instructional materials for many other texts, including *Literature: Reading Fiction, Poetry, Drama, and the Essay* (DiYanni, Random House); *Reading Fiction: An Anthology of Short Stories* (DiYanni, Random House); and *Reading Poetry: An Anthology of Poems* (DiYanni, Random House).

Reading Drama

AN ANTHOLOGY OF

PLAYS

TEACHER'S GUIDE